DESTINY
UNDER
FIRE

DESTINY UNDER FIRE

Copyright © 2017 by Patrick I. Odigie

ISBN: **ISBN-13: 978-0998792347**

Published by: Prophetic Power House Inc. New York
Editing
Funsho Balepo
Rosanda Richardson
Cover design by Divin Matthew
For more copies of this book and all our messages and training
materials please contact:
Patrick I. Odigie
Post Office Box 830, Uniondale NY 11553
516 499-2350

Email: propheticpowerhouse@yahoo.com
Website: www.patrickodigie.org

DESTINY
UNDER
FIRE

—— BY ——
PATRICK I. ODIGIE

Prophetic Power House Inc. New York

TABLE OF CONTENTS

Part 4
DREAM SOME MORE SOMEBODY!

Part 5
IF I PERISH, I PERISH

DEDICATION

I dedicate this book to all emerging generation of kingdom warriors who are battling through the frontline of the enemy with their end-time ministry and unique Destiny Design in Christ Jesus.Please with your torch burning brightly, keep your position in the ranks, remain under the blood stained banner of the gospel and remember that you have won, not because of what you can do, but because of whom you have chosen (Jesus the son of God). You are more than a conqueror.

FOREWORD.

Destiny under fire is a wow! It is electrifying, magnifying, and will keep every reader glued chapter by chapter; while keeping you at the edge of your seat! Above all, it will show you how to WIN irrespective of pressures and trials of life.

The glory of a 'Diamond in the rough' is covered until it is passed through intense fire, cutting, and polishing. Dr. Patrick Odigie has done an outstanding job to address the commonality of all destinies having the certainty of going under fire. Like a diamond in the rough, every destiny has a glory infused by God.

This dynamic man of God, Dr. Odigie, has revealed through this book - DESTINY UNDER FIRE that there is a price to pay; but that the PRIZE to be won IS WORTH THE PRICE to be paid!

Every Christian and all non-Christians need to get hold of this book, it will challenge and propel every reader that the only option despite the trials and difficulties of life is to

WIN. The battle is not over until you WIN!

I am not surprised that God chose the author, Dr. Patrick Odigie to write DESTINY UNDER FIRE. I have witnessed the author gone through different fires of life and without wavering in his faith; the author came out shinning like diamonds. Through DESTINY UNDER FIRE, Dr. odigie shared the strategies to WINNING all forms of fires.

I am honored to foreword this book – DESTINY UNDER FIRE and I recommend both Christians and non-Christians to read it.

Anthonia Adeyeye D. Min *[Senior Pastor]*
Abundant Life Christian Center,
New York.

ACKNOWLEDGMENTS

People around you matter. They either keep you inspired or get you deflated and frustrated always.

Mabel…you keep me inspired and your love fires me on.

My children, thank you for enduring my dynamic ministry. You have paid a huge price- your reward is sure.

Pastors Funsho and Babs Balepo, your hard pushing have seen the book come to light, thank you.

Rosanda Richardson, my dear editor, thank you for taking the time and the pains to read through the manuscript. You are simply wonderful.

PREFACE

DESTINY UNDER FIRE

"... When you walk through the fires of oppression, you will not be burned up; the flames will not consume you. Isaiah 43:1-3 (Touch Point Bible) and again, in Psalms 66:10-12 ASV " For thou, O God, hast proved us: Thou hast tried us, as silver is tried. Thou broughtest us into the net; Thou layedst a sore burden upon our loins. Thou didst cause men to ride over our heads; We went through fire and through water, But thou broughtest us out into a wealthy place (a place of rich fulfillment)."

The Bible is replete with fire language, and this fire Language in the Bible can be both inviting and scaring at the same time depending on where we stand in God and what feeds our particular perspective. We read lines like ".Chosen in the furnace of affliction" about our divine refinement for His purpose through sufferings and again, "when thou passes through the Fire…" which implies that we will at some point pass through the fire. Fire experience is a matter of when and not if! Regardless of what we do or fail to do, they will come.

We are constantly between two fires the Bible affirms. The fire of God is burning, purifying and sanctifying our bodies, souls, motives and making our 'whole soul as it were, an offering to the Redeemer's name'. The devil's fire, on the other hand, is just as real to the true and ardent seeker of the Living God. This particular fire is one of intense and vehement hate; a furious fire intent on our complete annihilation but moderated by the surpassing hand of Providence can only end up burning our ropes of bondage and limitation. God has even promised to make us, His ministers, a flaming fire! Fire is, naturally our supernatural habitat so do not panic when you are thrust suddenly into the trying fires of life.

Do not be alarmed when you pass through the fire for God assures us we will not be burned. Why be so afraid of fire anyway, when our Father is the Consuming Fire who indwells Everlasting burnings! In this volume, I like to present you some perspectives about some men who came through these fires and went ahead to fulfill their destinies shinning like gold purified by fire.

The man Moses encountered God in a burning bush in the wilderness of Sinai and wondered why the bush is not consumed, but he was the bush on fire! This very bush, (Moses), is Destiny under fire. He's been under divine fire which is why Pharaoh's fire could not consume him. Life can be a bout of pressure caused by many reasons among them, fulfilling your purpose. To see your dreams fulfilled will cost you everything but the prize is worth the price. Moses was called to be a Deliverer, but the sentence of death greeted him upon arrival into this world. He suffered rejection from those who ought to applaud him. He became a fugitive running from the hands of his adoptive father. He survived forty long years of seeing his vision grow old and out of reach but satanic opposition can not abort God's plans.

Apostle Peter loved God and gave everything including his life to serve, but a crushing punch from the enemy hit him at a critical moment leaving him with a wounded memory but Jesus went to work, and Peter bounced back. You too will bounce back regardless of where you find yourself right now! Joseph was hated for his dreams, but he kept on dreaming through his rejections, betrayals, false accusation, and imprisonment, but his God-given dreams outclassed his opposition and gave him the Presidency of a mighty Nation without citizenship, green card or yellow card.

Queen Esther was a slave girl who rose to the pinnacle of Persian power. The moment came for her to risk all her gain and she testified saying; 'if I perish, I perish.' She was preserved and by daring faith, she saved her people and preserved the Messianic posterity on the earth.

The three Hebrew children were willing to defend the honor of their God with their very life choosing to burn rather than bow to other gods. These all endured fiery storms; overcoming their fears and focusing on the invisible. You too will see much trouble and sometimes fall, but you will rise again and win because you are a Destiny under Fire.

INTRODUCTION

L ife can be a bout of pressure caused by many reasons. Sometimes the pressures are related to family issues, Career, ministry, finances, health or just plain personal frustration, confusion, anger, wants and many more! Other times ignorance or lack of understanding of our proper roles and standing in life, may give us deep pressures. A lot of times we face these pressures trying to fulfill purpose. For a good period of our lives we will live as if we are in a pressure cooker or in the oven. This experience is repeated many times in different seasons while we live on this earth. I am glad to announce to you that it forms a part of our walk with God and there is nothing much we can do to avert these pressures; they come with growth in Christ and are actually helping to shape our roles in the divine design and fulfillment of Destiny. Never try to condemn yourself for it is not the end of life, and do not force yourself out of divine purpose but let the pressures fire you into knowing and walking with God more closely. The book of James says in James 3:1-6

You know that under pressure,
your faith-life is forced into the

open and shows its true colors.

So don't try to get out of anything prematurely. Let it do its work so you become mature and well-developed, not deficient in any way.

If you don't know what you're doing, pray to the Father. He loves to help. You'll get his help, and won't be condescended to when you ask for it.

Ask boldly, believingly, without a second thought. People who "worry their prayers" are like wind-whipped waves (Message Bible).

In this book we shall be looking at Destiny Under Fire. We will see the metaphor fire as connoted in the Bible and as relevant to our destiny - divine purpose. We will see why we need to fight the good, and already victorious fight of faith just as Bible characters we shall spotlight in this book who went all the way.

Part **1**

PROMISE KEPT

Chapter 1

DESTINY AND FIRE

Literarily the word destiny refers to the sequence of events that will necessarily happen to a particular person or thing in the future. A predetermined usually inevitable, or irresistible course of events. (Thesaurus. Com) Destiny for me means your destination, your ultimate or final outcome in life and death. Many people believe in prefixed destiny, good or bad. In other words, they reckon their lot in life to be a sort of fate accompli regardless of their personal input or otherwise (doing nothing). When destiny is viewed in the above context, it places total responsibility on providence who pre-arranged our lot in life. This can predispose people to readily accept undesirable circumstance of their lives.

For the believer in Christ, we also believe in a divinely pre-fixed destiny. However the Bible tells clearly that our final outcome will be good. Jeremiah 29:11 says

> **For I know the plans and thought that I have for you, says the Lord, thoughts and plans for welfare and peace and not for evil, to give you hope in your final outcome.**

To buttress this apostle Paul in the book of Ephesians 2:10 teaches that we have been wired for success, with certain ambitions, desires, drives to play particular roles in life. However, it is possible to get it right or miss it. I pray that we will all get it right in the name of Jesus. But based on God's word we have opportunities to make choices. We must continually ask ourselves what God has created us to be, check it out from time to time and also find out what can make us to miss this. Adam and Eve had the opportunity to be obedient but they disobeyed and a lot of things changed!

> **Proverbs 22: 8 *He who sows iniquity will reap calamity and futility, and the rod of his wrath (with which he smites others,) will fail.***

Proverbs 14:*23 in all labor there is profit, but idle talk leads only to poverty.*

Rev 20:13 *And the sea delivered up the dead who were in it, death and hades (the state of death or disembodied existence) surrendered the dead in them, and all were tried and their cases determined by what they had done (according to their motives, aims and works).*

Based on this understanding of a beautiful future and blissful eternal hope, we as believers in Christ do not subscribe to fatalistic notion and self-defeating platitudes, we know that God planned and designed us to win so we fight intelligently and intentionally every step of the way and this is what it means to fight the good fight of faith.

Fire.
According to Wikipedia, Fire is the process of combustion; the event of something burning; a rapid oxidation of a material in an exothermic chemical reaction which releases

heat and light and many other reaction products, not least of which are carbon dioxide and water – yes, steam.

Fire.
A pleasant servant but a ravaging destroyer if it gets out of control. It can burn with purpose or without one, and it can cook your food every bit as easily as it can consume your home... or *you*, for that matter.

Fire's many positive effects when put to good use can transform a tortuous day into a pleasant one and possibly even save lives. It can stimulate growth, light up a room, provide warmth from the fireplace on a cold winter's night, resuscitate life, forge your precious stones, and help to provide balance and maintenance for organic bionetworks the world over.

The heat from the sun for instance is what sustains physically all life on Planet Earth, fostering evaporation, condensation, and precipitation to create rain; empowering plants to create their own food until they become nourishment for creatures higher up the food chain; energizing reptiles and cold-blooded beasts with the vigor to go about their daily lives; warming the planet so the ice from the polar caps do not freeze the world over…

But that's fire being *nice*. Fire out of control will raze your business to the ground in moments, ruining your entire life's work; it can destroy the same meal it cooked if not stopped when it should be; it will consume a forest, overwhelm an army, or bring down a building; and it can devastate entire cities. Evidently the underlying element about fire that you need to know is that fire is most valuable to you when it is under control, when it is put to good use with a defined purpose, otherwise it is going to get out of hand and annihilate something that you hold dear.

The Bible refers to God as a *Consuming Fire*, and the thought of what this means makes me shiver in awe. I think about the sun and how it powers the earth, radiating heat from the flames on its surface, and I imagine it crashing into our little blue planet. *Terra Firma* would be obliterated in hours – no, *days!* – Before the two celestial bodies ever made physical contact. Perhaps 500 times the size of the earth, the heat of the sun makes Mercury and Venus, its two closest planets, uninhabitable for humans, so much so we're contemplating the colder Mars as our most likely annex if we overwhelm this world. That's the kind of heat the sun radiates; it is the same heat that, when softened, sustains life on the earth. To think that this ball of fire was created by hardly a word from Our God Who then comes around to introduce Himself as a *Consuming Fire* ! I am immediately gripped by a reverent fear for who He is and what He means by this statement.

> *"For our God is a consuming fire."* - **Hebrews 12:29**

> *"Take heed unto yourselves, lest ye forget the covenant of the LORD your God, which he made with you, and make unto you a graven image, or the likeness of anything, which the LORD thy God hath forbidden thee. For the LORD thy God is a consuming fire; even a jealous God."*
> - **Deuteronomy 4:23-24**

> *"Understand therefore this day, that the LORD thy God is*

6

he which goeth over before thee; as a consuming fire he shall destroy them, and he shall bring them down before thy face; so shalt thou drive them out, and destroy them quickly, as the LORD hath said unto thee."

- **Deuteronomy 9:3**

Our God is a Consuming Fire: an introduction. Every bit as easily as we say God is Love, God *is* a Consuming Fire – it's *who* and *what* He is.

Our God is a Consuming Fire: a threat. Should you ever forget who I am and what I have instructed you, should you ever fail to evoke the solemn pact which exists between you and Me... *I will consume you!*

Our God is a Consuming Fire: a promise – this Consuming Fire that I am will go before you and destroy every enemy who stands against you and against the promises I have made to you.

7

HE DWELLS IN EVERLASTING BURNINGS

He dwells in Everlasting Burnings! – (Isaiah 33:14)

Who among us shall dwell with the devouring fire? Who among us shall dwell with everlasting burnings? The Everlasting burnings speaks of the fiery throne of God Himself. God's love and extreme Holiness portrays this very attribute of fire. His love and holiness are eternal and unchanging. Those of us His children who love His appearing will stand before His Fiery throne, with our purified and glorified eternal bodies. His throne speaks of thunder, lightning and burning lamps of fire. This is our awesome eternal home; the very presence of Almighty God.

He is the Devouring Fire on Mt. Sinai – (Exodus 24:17)

The Israelites had been having encounter with God, God had invited Moses up the Mount Sinai and the glory of the Lord had rested on the mount. It was an awesome experience. According to Gill's exposition, the sight of the glory of the Lord was like devouring fire on the top of the mount; For when God spoke out of the cloud, the glory of the Lord flashed out like devouring fire; it was not devouring fire, but it was like it; it was like a great blaze of fire, which consumes all that is in its ways; it was such a large body of light, and so clear and bright, that it looked like devouring flames of fire; and being upon the top of the mount was very visible, and seen at a great distance in the eyes of the children of Israel throughout, their camp.

He escorts His Vanguard in a Pillar of Fire by Night. (Deuteronomy 9:19)
This Consuming Fire, capable of ending all of existence, is yet what preserves *everything* much like the sun preserves the earth. This Consuming Fire, promised to be on our side, is what goes before us to destroy those who resist us – it showcases the verity and versatility of our omnipotent God, and thus we begin to comprehend how various incarnations of this fire, at work with purpose on this earth, can bring about various results for or against us, depending on where we stand with our God.

Our God, a consuming fire, can work for us and against our enemies.

9

During the 40-year exodus of Israel from Egypt to Canaan, God was with them in that flaming pillar of fire by night and cloud by day (Exodus 13:21-22; Deuteronomy 1:33). And when the Egyptians attacked He moved in between Pharaoh's armed forces and Israel's vulnerable multitude to protect until He was ready to destroy the enemy (Exodus 14:19-20).

Our God, a consuming fire, can work to destroy those who oppose God, whether or not they are directly connected to us, as was the case with Sodom and Gomorrah when God simply got fed up with their malevolent ways (Genesis 19:24-25).

Our God, *the fire*, can simply be there as a revelation of His presence or fiery love; as at the Burning Bush which was not consumed when God spoke out of it to Moses (Exodus 3:2-4). It can appear upon us as indication of the manifest authority of God in our lives, as on the day of Pentecost when the early apostles were empowered by the Holy Spirit (Acts 2:1-4). It can be evidence of His approval, as with Elijah versus the 400 prophets of Baal on Mount Carmel (1 Kings 18:36-39).

But it can destroy us also if we venture out of the will of God or desecrate something that is holy unto Him, as was the case with Nadab and Abihu, sons of Aaron who offered strange fires on God's altar and were consumed by Him (Leviticus 10:1-2); as with Uzzah the well-meaning guard who touched the Ark of the Covenant at a time when God was angry (2 Samuel 6:6-7); and as it happened with Anannias and Sapphira, when they angered the Holy Spirit by lying to the apostles while God moved in the early Church (Acts 5:1-11). And yes, it can work *within* us to consume all that is flawed and defective in order to reveal that which is perfect (Matthew 3:21).
But there are other fires.

There are *human fires* which may mean absolutely nothing, and which may or may not be accepted by God – such as the fires of Cain and Abel (Genesis 4:3-5); or the fire of Manoah and his wife, parents of Samson (Judges 18:15-20).

11

There are *strange fires*, which anger God and can bring about indignation and ruin – such as Nadab and Abihu's strange fires that brought about their death (Leviticus 10:1-2

THE FIRE OF THE ENEMY

Apostle Paul in his teachings emphasize about quenching the fiery darts of the enemy with the shield of faith. We must never assume that the enemy is sane, No he is not. In his possession is all manners of weapons of attack. A shield of faith is very important.

There is the *fire of the enemy*, whose only aim is to hurt us, but for this reason God has completely fired proofed us in Christ so that every satanic fire will only ultimately serve to destroy the enemy and his evil works in our lives (Isaiah 26:11). Isaiah 43:1-5

Then there is the *fire of hell*, a destruction which tends to result from wanton indiscretion with the tongue (James 3:6); and the fire of God's vengeance, God's final judgment against evil and perdition at The End (2 Peter 3:7-12).

We must be careful in this world not to

mistake strange fires or distractions for the Real Thing because that can bring about rapid destruction too. They can all look the same at first, but the purpose of them and the fruits that they bear are often what make the difference. "By their fruits you shall know them...," Jesus intimates in Matthew 7:20-23, right before He teaches his disciples to *not* get distracted by prophesies and wonderful works. The way to know that it is the fire of God which is burning within us is if we keep our gaze on Jesus through it all; if we look for Him inside of the flames.

"And ye shall seek me, and find *me*, when ye shall search for me with all your heart," says Jeremiah 29:13, which is exactly what Elijah did at Horeb which allowed him to know when it was God speaking, and also to know that God was not in the strong wind, or in earthquake, or in the fire, but in the still small voice. It is a function of what we are looking for that will determine what we find when we walk through a fire. If we are living and looking for God, He will reveal Himself to us in those flames. But if we are distracted, looking for self-will, human glory, or just excitement, we would be lost already.

"The thief cometh not but for to steal, to kill,

13

and to destroy," says John 10:10. This is what the fire of the enemy will do if we are caught up in it. The fire of the enemy comes to take away and destroy all that we have, even down to our very lives – our souls. But "I am come that they might have life, and that they might have *it* more abundantly."

The fire of God comes to give life, to refine us, to improve us, and to make us better. Just like the fire which cooks our food, it is not likely an experience that is palatable to endure while it lasts, but its purpose is to perfect us. What we need to understand about God is that because He is the source of all things, He can and does use fire in the manner that pleases Him, often for our own good. In Isaiah 48:10, God speaks about choosing us in the furnace of affliction, implying that affliction may come – which is never pleasant to experience – but out of it God can and does refine us in preparation for what He has purposed to do in our lives.

> *"When thou passes through the waters, I will be with thee; and through the rivers they shall not overflow thee: when thou walks through the fire, thou shalt not be burned;*

14

neither shall the flame kindle upon thee."
-        Isaiah 43:2

"...When thou walks through the fire, thou shalt not be burned..."
It is a two-pronged promise. First that we *WILL* at some time or other walk through some fire which has the potential to hurt us. Secondly, that *WHENwe do*, that fire will not be able to burn or consume us, and its flames will not even be able to kindle upon us – it will not be able to stay on our bodies.

_____

There is the fire of God which purifies and perfects, sanctifying our bodies, souls, and motives, giving us life and imbuing us with power; and there also is the fire of the enemy, kindled for the primary purpose of stealing, killing, and destroying great things in us.

_____

The Bible promises that we will encounter these fires inevitably in our walk on Planet Earth, so that we are constantly between two fires. The fire of God on the one hand, and on

15

the other the devil's fire, just as real to the true and ardent seeker of the Living God, but a furious fire of intense and vehement hate, intent upon our complete annihilation, moderated only by surpassing hand of Providence, so that it can only end up burning our ropes of bondage and limitation.

We are called to journey through both of these fires as we seek to fill our roles in God's destiny design for our lives. We must pass the test of both fires and come out refined and fine-tuned for God's purposes as necessitated by the will and zeal of the Lord. Enduring the discomfort for the necessary duration is essential for our journey to perfection. Though these burning and purifying fires, are uncomfortable much of the time, they work to make our whole soul as it were an offering to the redeemer's name.Hebrews 12:6-12 has this to say:

> *"For whom the Lord loves he chasteneth, and scourges every son whom he receives. If ye endure chastening, God dealeth with you as with sons; for what son is he whom the father chasteneth not? But if ye be without chastisement,*

16

whereof all are partakers, then are ye bastards and not sons.

"Furthermore we have had fathers of our flesh which corrected us, and we gave them reverence: shall we not much rather be in subjection unto the Father of spirits, and live? For they verily for a few days chastened us after their own pleasure; but he for our profit, that we might be partakers of his holiness.

"Now no chastening for the present seemeth to be joyous, but grievous: nevertheless, afterward it yieldeth the peaceable fruit of righteousness unto them which are exercised thereby.

Picture then a *Destiny Under Fire!* This is the meal being cooked with a purpose. God has promised to make us, His ministers a flaming fire! But this often requires that we pass through the fire ourselves, and it is never a comfortable experience.

Chapter 2

THE MAN AT THE BURNING BUSH

"Now Moses kept the flock of Jethro his father in law, the priest of Midian: and he led the flock to the backside of the desert, and came to the mountain of God, even to Horeb. And the angel of the Lord appeared unto him in a flame of fire out of the midst of a bush: and he looked, and, behold, the bush burned with fire, and the bush was not consumed.

"And Moses said, I will now turn aside, and see this great sight, why the bush is not burnt. And when the Lord saw that he turned aside to see, God called unto him out of the midst of the bush, and said,

Moses, Moses. And he said, here am I. And he said, Draw not nigh hither: put off thy shoes from off thy feet, for the place whereon thou standest is holy ground. Moreover he said, I am the God of thy father, the God of Abraham, the God of Isaac, and the God of Jacob. And Moses hid his face; for he was afraid to look upon God."

- **Exodus 3:1-6**

I have always been fascinated by God's sense of the theatrical – He hardly ever does the same thing twice, but they always all point to the one thing: His purpose and glory. I remember a portion of scripture where an angel of the Lord descended upon an oppressing army from Assyria and completely destroyed them. Sennacherib their king awakened the next morning to the sight of a hundred and eighty-five thousand corpses, and promptly fled to his home country, only to be assassinated by his own sons (2 Kings 19). This same God it was who decided to drown all of Pharaoh's army in the Red Sea (Exodus 14). And still it was He who raised an ambushment against the children of Ammon,

Moab, and Mount Seir *"utterly to slay and destroy"* one another (2 Chronicles 20).

We've seen Him come in the flesh as Jesus, descend from heaven like a dove or cloven tongues of flame as the Holy Spirit, stand like a soldier beside Joshua, and speak out of a still small voice to the soul-weary Prophet Elijah. And this time, He chose to speak to Moses from out of a burning bush – one that while being licked by flames would still not be consumed.

No, we do not always know why God does what He does, but sometimes He leaves crumbs for us to follow so that the diligent minds can find them.

> **"The secret things belong unto the Lord our God: but those things which are revealed belong unto us and to our children forever, that we may do all the words of this law."** Deuteronomy 29:29

> **"It is the glory of God to conceal a thing: but the honour of kings is to search out a matter."** - Proverbs 25:2

20

So, when we ponder why God would so appear to Moses and not to anyone else that we know of in scripture it makes us look a little closer – for there is a purpose to everything that God does. We understand from 1 Corinthians 10:1-2 that the passage through the red sea was symbolic of baptism, and that the Feast of the Passover is prophetic toward the coming and sacrifice of Jesus. But having seen Jesus stand beside Joshua, a soldier, as a soldier Himself; David, a shepherd, declare that *"the Lord is my Shepherd"*, we begin to wonder – perhaps God reveals Himself to us in terms of what we can understand or in terms of what He is symbolizing.

This man, Moses, was at this point in his life, 80 years of age and no longer an inexperienced child. Having been forgotten in the wilderness 40 long years tending sheep and having previously lived as a prince in the world's leading civilization of the day. Thereafter he fled for his life after ill-advisedly acting to defend his people against the treacherous rule of his adoptive father,

21

treading through the desert on foot.

This was a man who had been through an intense fire but still standing – *barely*, but still there. Could it just be, that God was symbolizing to this man that this was his very own life? Could it be that God was telling Moses things about himself right there and then that he could not have known – that the fact that he had been through hell and high water by no means implied that he was done and dusted? That the flames he had endured had only served to burn off the chaff and imperfections in his life, only to bring him out refined? Moses after all was later referred to by the Lord as the meekest human being on the planet after he had begun his work in service of God.

Moses had been through the fire of affliction and was likely a broken man in his mind – the throne room and luxuries of Egypt a distant memory in his long lost past. His guilt and the futility of his efforts to aid his people must have weighed like a log in his mind. He was getting up there in age, had a few sheep which belonged to his wife's daddy, and was probably resigned to his lot in life. To think that God was only just beginning with his life…!

The bush was burning and not consumed because that very bush was MOSES himself – his Destiny Under Fire. It was a fire of his own making, he may have thought. He had become a fugitive in self-exile himself after going against the man he called 'Father', and failing.

It was a fire kindled out of the elements of nature, his mind could have fancied. Here he was, a victim of circumstances, sequestered in the backside of the desert, tending sheep in the scorching glare of the sun. The pickings were perhaps slim, but it was a living – barely.

But it was a fire that the Lord had chosen to put to positive use, to purify and perfect a man in preparation for an assignment so significant that much of the Old Testament hinged on its success. It had never been just him, by him, or *about* him – it had always been about God's divine purpose. See, even his life was never really *his*! From before he was born, God purposed Moses' life carefully to begin to

23

herald the fulfillment of His grand plan for deliverance – not just of Israel, but of the entire world.

> *"And [God] said unto Abram, know of a surety that thy seed shall be a stranger in a land that is not theirs, and shall serve them; and they shall afflict them four hundred years; and also that nation, whom they shall serve, will I judge: and afterward they shall come out with great substance."*
> -   **Genesis 15:13-14**

It had been God's grand design that Israel would be in bondage of affliction for a duration of four hundred years, and then He would bring them out in freedom. Through the early chapters of the Book of Exodus, we find this design gradually unfolding, and in the middle of it affliction. Pharaoh plotted to have all male children of the Hebrews murdered at birth, in his own reasoning to keep the Children of Israel from ever getting strong enough to challenge or refute them, and his fears weren't entirely unfounded – God was working to bring them out of that bondage.

And so we find the suffering of Israel multiply, as did the death of their children. Yet, in the midst of it the Levite, Amram, took the maiden Jochebed to wife and had three children: Miriam, Aaron, and Moses, whilst the streets of Goshen ran red with the blood of Hebrew infants. The youngest of these three was to be the tool that God would use to work out the deliverance he promised to Abram some 400 years prior.

I find it hard to imagine that anyone is not captivated by the parallels drawn by this story to that of the birth of Jesus, and with hindsight the deliverance that He was bringing into the world. We all have been slaves to sin since... *forever*, and God has purposed to set us free from that debilitating bondage. His plan was Jesus, and when Jesus was born, the streets of Bethlehem and Judea ran red with the blood of infants two years old and younger. (Matthew 2: 13-18) Yet Jesus, rather like Moses in a basket, was ferried by his parents to faraway Egypt for the duration of 3 to 4 years.

A clear and undeniable purpose in everything that God does.

Moses may have thought it as coincidence at work in his life, growing up in the halls of Pharaoh's palace, nurtured however by his own mother with a paycheck from the treasury; observing his people suffer, at the same time learning what it meant to rule and lead a people.

God can busy Himself with the details of our life's circumstances without our conscious awareness and later use every previous experience in our lives to His own glory.

I imagine that the soul-rending pain of watching the people who were his people going through that kind of suffering would perhaps mirror the agony that Jesus felt when he walked this earth and saw us all in bondage to the devil, whose only purpose was to steal, kill, and destroy – a determined ruler of this world who had purposed to steal our joy, destroy our livelihood, and eventually kill us, before he would let us even come close to seeing the salvation that Jesus was destined to bring us. Moses could not stop himself; one day he struck and killed a man.

It was a presumptuous action. His agony was real and it was there for a purpose; but killing Egypt one soldier at a time was not that purpose. His guilt drove him out into the wilderness, and he was requisitioned in that barren oven for another 40 years until he was baked enough and God was ready to put him to use.

While he went through it, he was initially incensed at his people's suffering. Later he became impatient and impertinent. Finally, he resigned to his fate because he no longer was in position to do and be all that God had intended – something that he could sense in his heart but perhaps could not put his finger on. How it makes sense when God says His thoughts are not our thoughts and His ways are not our ways…. For when Moses thought it was over, it was just beginning!

But all along Moses was merely being baked in preparation for what God was going to assign unto him. He did not know it at the time, but all along Moses had been under divine fire not of his own making which is why Pharaoh's fire cannot consume him. The scorch of the desert, the fear of Pharaoh, the palace upbringing, the basket in the Nile, and

27

the death of so many babies – it was all a bush burning, yet a bush that was not consumed.

> *"...Put off thy shoes from off thy feet, for the place whereon thou standest is holy ground."*
> *- Exodus 3:5*

God had always been there behind the scenes, watching Moses' life carefully and painstakingly, a refiner sitting at his fire, conscientiously observing and inspecting, scrutinizing every occurrence and event – a flame burning – but never permitting any one of them to destroy the work of art that He was patiently molding in the fires of affliction.

> *"And he shall sit as a refiner and purifier of silver: and he shall purify the sons of Levi, and purge them as gold and silver, that they may offer unto the LORD an offering of righteousness."* **Malachi 3:3**

Hope you didn't miss it in there... that last line. The reason God is taking us through all of these, is that we as gold, silver, or other precious stones are refined by the divine flame so that we can become that prized and pleasant *offering of righteousness* UNTO HIMSELF! Beloved, if it has been said once, it has been said half a million times. Your life does not belong to you. Jesus at the cross paid the ultimate price in order to buy you out of the bondage of sin that Satan had placed upon you through the blood of Adam which originally flowed through your veins, making it impossible to approach or have a relationship with God.

> ***"For by him were all things created, that are in heaven, and that are in earth, visible and invisible, whether they be thrones, or dominions, or principalities, or powers: all things were created by him, and for him."***
>
> **- Colossians 1:16**

Let's get that out of the way first and foremost – God created everything for Himself, by Himself, and in order to bring pleasure *to Himself*. But through the fall of Adam we all got lost and bound to Satan, slaves to sin. And like Israel in Egypt, there was no getting away from it because this taskmaster was purposed to *end* us before he would let any of us go free.

29

"Behold, I was shapen in iniquity; and in sin did my mother conceive me."
- **Psalm 51:5**

In that state you and I, were truly lost, owned completely by the devil and purposed for destruction. That was when Jesus stepped in and offered Himself, a sacrifice for our sins – my life for theirs. You can have me and do with me what you will. Only then, you must let them go. Knowing that there was no way out, Jesus gave Himself up to be the price paid – the *propitiation for our sins*.

"And he is the propitiation for our sins: and not for ours only, but also for the sins of the whole world."
- **1 John 2:2**

"Herein is love, not that we loved God, but that he loved us, and sent his son to be the propitiation of our sins."
- **1 John 4:10**

God loves us, but the choice is entirely ours.

30

Through Jesus the price was paid and the chains were loosened, but we get to decide if we want to accept Him and walk with Him out of that bondage into freedom. Having paid that price and if we accepted it though, we don't belong to ourselves anymore, but to Him. And from that point on, everything we live for is so that He can perfect Himself in us. Even from before we are born He begins to work things out in order to fulfil that purpose. When we wander out of that purpose, He chastens us, because we belong to Him.

CHAPTER 3

WHAT DO YOU DO WHILE
UNDER FIRE?

W hat then do you do when you are struck with the fire of affliction? Run? Tremble? Stare it boldly in the face?

"Now therefore, behold, the cry of the children of Israel is come unto me: and I have also seen the oppression wherewith the Egyptians oppress them. Come now therefore, and I will send thee unto Pharaoh, that thou mayest bring forth my people the children of Israel out of Egypt. And Moses said unto God, Who am I, that I should go unto Pharaoh, and that I should bring forth the children of Israel out of Egypt?

> ***And he said, Certainly I will be
> with thee; and this shall be a
> token unto thee, that I have
> sent thee: When thou hast
> brought forth the people out of
> Egypt, ye shall serve God upon
> this mountain."***
> -   **Exodus 3:1-12**

Scripture is not vague about this at all if you really desire to know – *and do* – the truth. Right there in that passage in Exodus we can see it in Moses' reaction...
-        Exodus 3:4-6

When God called to Moses out of the burning bush, the very next thing that happens tells us what next we should do. In the very next sentence the Lord says:

> **"*I am the God of thy father, the
> God of Abraham, the God of
> Isaac, and the God of Jacob.*"**

A lot of the time we miss this simple little reality that is glaring at us simply because we are awed by the unusual happening around us, but this is not meant to be. The first thing we

33

want to do when we are faced with a fire is to identify the kind of fire that it is, where it has come from, which will go some ways in determining the *purpose* of that fire. It is only then that we should determine what we are meant to do with that fire – ignore it, resist it, or surrender to it. But we are by no means to surrender to a fire when we do not know it's source.

"And no marvel; for Satan himself is transformed into an angel of light."
- 2 Corinthians 11:14

"Beloved, believe not every spirit, but try the spirits whether they are of God: because many false prophets are gone out into the world. Hereby know ye the Spirit of God: Every spirit that confesseth that Jesus Christ is come in the flesh is of God: And every spirit that confesseth not that Jesus Christ is come in the flesh is not of God: and this is that spirit of antichrist, whereof ye

34

**have heard that it should
come; and even now already is
it in the world."** *- 1 John 4:1-3*

Even the devil himself can present himself to
you with every conceivable fanfare to
convince you that he is an angel of light, and if
your eye is not focused on the right things you
will miss it entirely. I shiver at the thought of
religions and sects that are born out of people
who claim to have encountered spiritual
beings that told them things which came to
pass, or that gave them access to powers
imaginable. This by no means implies that
they are from God because Satan is himself a
master at deceiving people. In order to
experience God, you have to be looking for
Him; you have to be interested in finding *Him*,
or else you will find something else and you
can end up selling your soul to it.

Yes, the devil can craft a fire that appears to
have every conceivable characteristic of what
you *think* should be God so that you would be
very inclined to believe him. The passage in 1
John 4:1-3 is priceless in dealing with this:
"*do not believe every spirit.*" Instead, you
want to employ these five mutually inclusive

35

and interrelated keys to dealing with such a situation:

   a) **Know your** *Word.* There are certain characteristics about a spiritual encounter that you can identify from merely knowing what the Bible says about a situation; and knowing what the Bible says about such a situation will also prepare you to address and deal with that situation. Three times Jesus was tempted by the devil in the wilderness, and three times Jesus gave the devil the best kind of answer you can conjure up: *"It is written…"*

Please friend, where is your *"It is written…?"* Do you know it? Do you *speak* it? You're setting yourself up for a rude shock if you don't know and speak the Word. Some folks carry their *Word* about in their pockets without ever reading it. Some hold on to the Bible whenever they feel they are under some kind of spiritual presence or experience. Sorry folks, it doesn't work that way.

   b) **Speak the** *Word.* It is not enough to know the scriptures. That *Word* is powerless to you unless you speak it, and well, you can't speak what you don't know. You could carry a million Bibles around with you, build your house in the shape of a cross, or even carry half a gazillion cisterns of special 'holy water' in your basement, but if you never open that Bible, read those words, and know them by heart enough to speak them when you are in a situation, trust me when I say that you are not likely to come out of the situation the way that you are supposed to – *victorious*.

"*This book of the law shall not depart out of thy mouth; but thou shalt meditate therein day and night, that thou mayest observe to do according to all that is written therein: for then thou shalt make thy way prosperous, and then thou shalt have good success.*"

- Joshua 1:8

It really is that simple. You don't let the Book – the *Word* – ever *not* be in your mouth. The way to do this is to *meditate* on – read it and think on it – day and night; and then observe to *do* it – act according to the precepts that are written in it. That is how you will make your way

37

prosperous and have *good* success.

Clearly, if there is such a thing as *good* success, there must be *bad* success as well, if the Bible is being so crystal clear about it. Say you set out to kill a guy and you succeeded in killing the guy that *is* success. But you shouldn't have been trying to kill a man in the first place, so that kind of success is bad. When you succeed at something you aren't meant to be doing, that's bad success. When you fall for the trap set by an evil spirit masquerading as an angel of light, even though you get a billion ardent followers from all over, you have failed in God's book.

c) **Do the *Word*.** Know the word. Speak it. Do it. If you read your Bible as diligently as you should, the next time the devil presents you with a strange fire you can be instant, in season, out of season…
   "Preach the word; be instant in season, out of season; reprove, rebuke, exhort with all long suffering and doctrine."
   -        1 Timothy 4:2

But we are also challenged as described in

Joshua 1:8 to live according to the things that are written in the *Word*. Doing the Word means surrendering to it and living our lives based on the things that are spelt out in it. This is what makes us *living* sacrifices, holy and acceptable to God. This is then what empowers our actions...

> **"Submit yourselves therefore to God. Resist the devil, and he will flee from you."**
> - James 4:7

I like the movie *War Room* which brilliantly illustrates this passage in action. A lot of preachers sometimes say: "*Resist the devil, and he will flee from you,*" but I think they miss the crucial first line when they do. The devil doesn't just flee from anybody. If you aren't a child of God – if you haven't accepted Jesus Christ as your Lord and Saviour, you haven't been given the power and authority to be a child of God. The devil then has no inclination to flee from you simply because you resisted him. He can laugh in your face and there'd be nothing you can do about it.

Do the *Word* in obedience; this is your reasonable service, your submission to the

39

will of God. It is from this submitted perch that you can exercise the authority to resist the devil and he will have nothing else to do than to flee.

> *d)* ***Challenge that fire and the spirit behind it***. Speaking of *speaking* the word, when you are faced with a situation that looks divine, your first objective is to look for God in that situation. A strange fire can burn with the same intensity as the real thing, but its purpose and end result tend to be different than what God does. God preserves, the devil destroys. The devil breeds fear; God gives us power, love, and soundness of mind.

The Bible in our passage from 1 John 4 urges us to *try* every spirit if it will acknowledge Jesus as Son of God and Messiah. When a spirit is not able or willing to do this, it is not of God. That's how simple it is.

See, too many people have been fooled by the impressive, but even Jesus warns against this. The devil can do tricks too. In Matthew 7:21-23.

"*Not every one that saith unto*

40

me, Lord, Lord, shall enter into the kingdom of heaven; but he that doeth the will of my Father which is in heaven. Many will say to me in that day, Lord, Lord, have we not prophesied in thy name? and in thy name have cast out devils? and in thy name done many wonderful works? And then will I profess unto them, I never knew you: depart from me, ye that work iniquity."
- Matthew 7:221-23

They come excited about the miracles that they have done, some of them even using the Name of Jesus. They come bragging about the prophecies that they have given, some of which came to pass with startling alacrity. They come declaring about the devils they cast out of people; the mighty crusades; the enormous churches they built and the crowds they pulled; but Jesus called them workers of iniquity.

It is a sobering thought, but it is not that farfetched from the life and times of Elijah, whom we have mentioned in passing earlier. Out there on the holy mount – mind, he *was* on

41

the *holy* mountain, Hebron – many mighty and wonderful things were happening around him. The wind, the storm, the earthquake and the fire, but the prophet was looking for evidence of his God and he saw Him in none of those mighty looking events and occurrences. And because he was truly interested in finding God, when God spoke up he recognized his voice, listened, and obeyed. These were Jesus' precise words to His disciples:

> *"And the seventy returned again with joy, saying, Lord, even the devils are subject unto us through thy name. And he said unto them, I beheld Satan as lightning fall from heaven. Behold, I give unto you power to tread on serpents and scorpions, and over all the power of the enemy: and nothing shall by any means hurt you. Notwithstanding in this rejoice not, that the spirits are subject unto you; but rather rejoice, because your names are written in heaven."*
> Luke 10:17-20

His point: not that those things are wrong,

they're just not the point. Those signs follow you *because* you believe, but they are not the reason *why* you believe. You believe by faith, because God reveals Himself by the Holy Spirit into your heart. So don't get stuck on the signs – look for God in them. God doesn't want to destroy; He doesn't want any to perish. Jesus paid a dire price for every soul on the planet and He is not eager to see anyone fail to accept His gift. This is why He continues to give us rope after rope to pull, peradventure we will eventually accept Him and surrender to Him. Willingly.

Any spirit, fire, or apparition, that is too eager to show off, to kill, or to destroy is not of God. Add to that any spirit that is too eager to accept your worship. God's angels *don't* let you worship them because as a human being you are senior to them, especially if you have accepted Jesus as Lord and Saviour. Besides they know the danger of trying to share glory that is intended only for God. They defer all praise to Him and join you even to give it.

> *"And Manoah said unto the angel of the LORD, I pray thee, let us detain thee, until we shall have made ready a kid for thee.*

43

And the angel of the LORD said unto Manoah, Though thou detain me, I will not eat of thy bread: and if thou wilt offer a burnt offering, thou must offer it unto the LORD. For Manoah knew not that he was an angel of the LORD."
-          Judges 13:15-16

"And I John saw these things, and heard them. And when I had heard and seen, I fell down to worship before the feet of the angel which shewed me these things. "
-          Revelations 22:8

It really doesn't get much clearer than that. Even Jesus while He walked this earth would only take so much praise from people around Him, asking them not to call Him 'good' because only God deserved that honor (Matthew 19:16-17); and the apostles while they did their pilgrimage across the then-known world, they would not let the people worship them (Acts 14:13-15).
Challenge the Spirit. Ask him who he is. If he does not reverence Jesus, that fire is not from

44

God. Even if it looks beautiful today, it will turn around and destroy you. Knowing this, God introduced Himself first to Moses before instructing him.

The same thing happened with Gideon when the angel appeared unto him to give him the assignment to take down his father's strange altar and lead Israel against the Midianites (Judges 6). The angel took its time to introduce himself, and while Gideon continued to doubt and fear, it patiently gave him sign after Sign until the once-timid mighty-man-of-valour could stand with confidence and follow the instructions given him to the glory of God.

Don't be afraid to inquire the source and nature of the fire you see burning before you. God is not too timid to introduce Himself to you. As a matter of fact, He *wants* to introduce Himself: Yahweh. Jehovah. The God of Abraham, Isaac, and Jacob. He does this with so many mighty men in scripture. You can ask Him for signs too, so that you can be sure. Don't worry, He won't consume you, so long as you're doing it because you deliberately want to know, not because you want to be tempting God.

45

e) **Do obeisance.** Once you know who you are faced with – that it is God at work on your behalf, the next thing you need to do as someone encountering a fire is obeisance. Job did. Daniel did. John the Beloved Apostle, Jeremiah the Prophet, Abraham...

"Humble yourselves in the sight of the Lord, and he shall lift you up."
It is a privilege to experience the fire of God at work in your life, and it is a privilege that you want to hold in high regard. Humble yourself before God once you know Who it is before Whom you stand. This is a priceless privilege that many have spent their lifetimes and livelihoods trying to find but failed.

"Moses hid his face; for he was afraid to look upon God."
(Exodus 3:6)

2 Samuel 5:17-25 describes a story of Philistines attacking David shortly after he became king over Israel. I find it interesting that the first day they attacked, David inquired of God and God told him to face them head-on. He did, and triumphed greatly. Shortly afterwards, the Philistines attacked again and

46

this time when David inquired of God, he was told not to go against them head on, but to go around them and wait for a certain signal before striking them from behind.

This is God; you don't predict Him – you can't; so stop trying to. When Christ walked the earth He hardly did a miracle the same way twice. One blind man he spat on and asked, "Can you see?" The man replied, "Yes, I see men like trees." Jesus laid hands on this time and then the man could see (Mark 8:22-26). Another blind man he asked, "What do you want?" Bartimaeus said he wanted his eyesight back, and Jesus said, "Receive your sight" (Mark 10:46-52). Then a third blind man Jesus made mud with spittle and told to go wash his face at a pool (John 9:1-7).

Three instances, same miracle, three different ways. You can't put God in a straightjacket. What you want to do is listen to what He is saying to you *today*. Don't assume that He is giving you the same instruction as yesterday. Yesterday's evils were yesterday's, today has its own to be dealt with. Listen. Then obey. That is how the fires will not kindle upon you and you will not be burned.

47

Recognize this: often God manifests Himself to us by symbolic means that are unique to us and may not be understood by anyone else. For this reason, you should not expect that the way God spoke with your dad or with your pastor is the same way He's going to speak to you. He could, and He could choose not to. You have to be open to Him, and you have to be looking for Him, otherwise you will not find Him at all.

In addition, not every fire that you experience is fire from the Lord, but all of it is fire that the Lord can use – so do not despair. You do have to be looking for Him in that fire though, or it might confuse, mislead, or consume you. When you're looking for Him don't get caught up in the fanfare and distractions – the devil can do those too. Look for humility; look for kindness and gentleness; look for love and peace – this is what God offers today. Yes, He is a consuming fire, but we live in an era of grace today, one in which our Father in Heaven does not desire to see anyone perish. Because we are not humanly able to live up to His high standards, He uses Jesus through grace to offer His love.

When you recognize God in the flames of your affliction, humble yourself before Him. *"By grace you are saved through faith, not of works lest any man should boast.*" You have not done anything of your own self to *make* Him reach out to you; He reached out to you because He loves you and wants to save you. Don't get pompous and feel like you are better than any other person. In English, you aren't; it's just grace at work in your life. Humble yourself before God so that He can lift you high in His own time and way.

(f)**Listen.** Don't run ahead of yourself simply because you think you *know* God. You may have read the entire Bible but believe me when I say you don't understand anything in it without the help of the Holy Spirit, and what He is teaching you today may be a lesson totally different from what He took you through yesterday. *Listen.* Understand what you can about whatever you're being taught or instructed. Then obey. Unequivocally. Unreservedly. Without hesitation. Without doubt. Then He will lead you by the hand and perfect in *and with* your life what He has intended. And then when you catch the vision, when you *know* the revelation, *run with it!*

Chapter 4

FIGHT THE GOOD FIGHT OF FAITH

Once a man comes in contact with God's grace and realties and he is sure that the fire is from God, he must go all the way to fight the good fight. You should not be afraid to fight for your right .If you do not rise up and go all the way as you should once you have caught the vision, your fate can only be the same as the individual who is trying to run without a vision or direction from God.

It is sad to say, but also painfully true; some of us have been battling from a weak position, which is never a good place to be, especially for a person of destiny. A weak position is a place of ignorance and directionless. Like a man setting out on a journey without knowing where he is going or having anyone to lead him. Abraham had God's Word and assurance, and indeed when he got to where God wanted to show him, God told Abraham to look out as far as his eyes could see. But imagine if he didn't know where he was going, and he didn't have anyone leading him. Good old Father Abraham could have been walking for eons without ever knowing when or where to stop!

A weak position is a place without grace. Grace which is the only essence that has the capacity to save us since our own physical capacity is grossly inadequate; and we tap into grace by the use of faith, since the Bible clearly says that we are saved by grace *through faith*. A weak position is a place without faith!

> *"For by grace are ye saved through faith; and that not of yourselves: it is the gift of God:"*
> -   Ephesians 2:8

> *"But without faith it is impossible to please him: for he that cometh to God must believe that he is, and that he is a rewarder of them that diligently seek him."*
> -   Hebrews 11:6

There is a good fight, there is a bad fight.

There is a fight of faith – it's a good fight; and there is a fight outside of faith – a bad one. You know that you are fighting outside of faith when there is an absence of grace. When you are fighting outside of faith grace goes on vacation and the situation becomes a large overbearing cross. You are outside the cycle of God's plan and the enemy appears to be overwhelmingly powerful. Because you're fighting by yourself. Something has gone wrong! It becomes your own battle – against an enemy you cannot hope to overcome, as he is vastly more experienced than you are.

> *When you fight in your divine placement, in God's placement, your divine arena, that kind of battle is not your battle; it's the Lord's.*

This by no means implies that you are not going to fight. It certainly does not imply that because you are in the will of God there will be smooth sailing all the way… no struggles, no opposition... No!
The good land, the large land, the land flowing with milk and honey, the one which has your name on it was already possessed by Jebusites, Hittites, Perizzites, Canaanites,

52

Amorites and all the other "ites", all ready for the kill, determined to stop you from taking back from them what is rightfully yours (Deuteronomy 7:1). In real terms these are the joys and pleasures purposed for you by God; your health, prosperity, and success; your up-liftment and promotion; and without question, your peace of mind and dominion over all that God has created.

> *"But as many as received him, to them gave He power to become the sons of God, even to themthat believe on His name:"*
> - John 1:12

It's all yours – the devil has no right to touch any of it though he touches them anyway. If we do not know that they are rightfully ours, or if we do not know that we have the power and authority to take them back (by grace, through faith), or if we do not exercise our faith and actively *take them back.*

I love the scriptures in the Bible which says, *"Lift up your heads, oh ye gates and even lift them up ye everlasting doors and the King of Glory*.... Every time I read that, I love it – and

53

it says "*this is the generation of them that seek Him....Jacob. Selah.*" (Psalm 24). We *are* that generation – the generation of those who send notice to the devil: "We will not back off; *we do not*!

Back home where I am from before coming to settle in the United States, we at one time had to deal with a brand new generation of hardened armed robbers, the kinds who write a letter which goes something like: "August 12, at 7 or 8 p.m., we are coming to pay you a visit. We would like to advise you. Be a gentleman, keep our money. And be wise enough to keep the police out of it."

And there would be pretty little the police can do about it indeed, because these were some of the most hardboiled hoodlums anyone ever came across: desperate, focused, and packing plenty more firepower than even the military. The police were no good in such a situation; back then folks simply folded their hands and did exactly what was demanded of them in order to keep life and limbs together.

Thank God I don't hear much about that kind of thing anymore. I recall a story I was told once, about a certain man who got one such letter and went to the police to report it, dropping the letter with them for reference and filing, confident they would protect him. The noble gentlemen-on-the-road did show up when and how they promised, so the man in question ran off unto the roof, leaving his two daughters behind.

Graciously they called out to him: "Please sir, come down. Is this not the letter we wrote to you? Why did you go to the police? Please give us our money and we will be on our merry way."

A very gentlemanly advice. Folks never messed with these kinds. A woman in a similar situation presented the hoodlums with all the funds at her disposal and she was told: "Is this all of the money? Are you not a Christian? Don't you go to church? Why are you hiding some of it? Madam please bring everything."

I am talking about wicked people on the wrong side of history – loaded, informed, and they either had law enforcement in their pockets or a very high placed rat in the precincts all around. But imagine someone standing up to them and saying: *"No, you cannot have what is mine, because it is mine!*

And that which you have taken, you must return immediately, with interest!"

We are not the wicked; we are the righteous. But nobody makes that kind of bold stand without the backing of something superior and beyond the human ken. It is not really a battle that we fight; it is a victory that was won for us by Jesus Christ at Calvary, and today we merely enforce it... *Grace, through faith.*

Nobody pursues the wicked yet he flees. But the righteous is as bold as a lion. Our righteousness is not of works, but by grace through faith. Authority has been given us by One Who Has Paid a dire and precious Price for all and sundry, our Lord who does not turn His back on any. Yet it is only those who have accepted Him who are able to tap into it.

We are always faced with opposition, yes we fight. But it's a good fight of faith. We are hardened believers. Persuaded. Fully conscious of who we are in Christ and precisely what we are doing – where we are going. And by grace through faith we stand up to face down any enemy, confident that not by power, nor by might, but by the Holy Spirit of the Living God we are laying our rightful claim upon a treasure won for us by One *"who filleth all in all"* (Ephesians 1:23).

There was a time in my life after a season of unprecedented blessing, I mismanaged the blessing, ran through the money, and was so broke I could barely put food on the table. The funny part was that for a good while I still did not know I was out of funds. Still giving testimonies, I was, handing out loads of cash and advances, until after a while those whom I loaned monies to weren't giving it back, and endless financial pressures began to mount like I had never seen them do before. It started to occur to me then that I was broke, and presently those who had been coming by to collect from me simply weren't coming anymore. *There was nothing to come to!*

I thank God for men of God, and I mean no disrespect as I say this difficult thing: like most everybody else when things are good they come by, and when things go awry many of them filter away just like regular people one may not expect so much from. It is quite pitiful that even men of God do gossip. And at this difficult time when it was just my faithful wife, my lovely children, and myself settling in to face the music of my mistakes, there were precious few of them around to offer anything other than their backs and their silence.

One of them did come back eventually, after a while, bringing money and yams – or was it plantains? I remember saying quite harshly to him that day, "Why did you come back? What did you come to do? Since you ran away, did I look for you? Do you know why? It's because I know who I am. I know where I am coming from. I know where I am now. And I know where I am going. Look at me straight in the eyes as I am telling you: I will get there."

It shook the man quite a bit. Then I said, "bring the yam."

Hey, I wasn't going to reject the tubers of yams. I needed them badly then.

At the point of his encounter with the burning bush, Moses was in a place of what I call Destiny Under Fire. Everything God promised him was like smoke. He was a man hiding from friends because he didn't have the ability at this time in his life to stand before friends. You may have experienced such yourself, or actually still be in it: That kind of time when you screen your phone calls or just let the phone keep ringing. Friends, family, loved ones, strangers and acquaintances alike – you don't want to take any calls because you can see the mess that your life looks like right now, and you know it is impossible to explain to anyone. You are not picking up because you are not up to it. I have been there before, and I wonder if you have also… That kind of time when you lack that courage to go into the midst of your friends, when you want to hide yourself even from your own shadow because what once looked like a great destiny has become no more than mere smoke… and you cannot dissociate yourself from it!

Moses was no ordinary man – he never was. From the very start he was a man with destiny, born to lead, raised in the palace by a princess; son of slaves, saved only by the mighty working hand of God; he had a burning passion in his heart for the plight of his people. Surely only God could have put it there, and of a certainty the mighty hand of God would strengthen his arm to battle the oppressive Egyptians if he had to fight them one at a time… But here was that same great Moses, prince of Egypt, commander of Pharaoh's armies, scourge of the tyrants of Africa and

59

Arabia, and song on the lips of the maidens on the Nile… leading sheep on the backside of the desolate wilderness for the past 40 years. Long lost and forgotten.

Moses was in a place of Destiny Under Fire, as you probably are as well today.
Let me declare to you:
You were born to lead.
God brought you forth for just such an hour.
You were not born to be a follower.
You are born to be a leader.
You are a leader of the people.
You are a leader of the people.
You are a leader of the people.

That is your destiny. But your great destiny may be under fire right now.
The devil loathed Moses so much that before he even arrived Satan had prepared a decree: "*dead on arrival*". Kill all the male children, by the mouth of the Pharaoh. But God said: not this one, as He does all the time for those He holds dear.

> **"*Saying, Touch not mine anointed, and do my prophets no harm.*"**
> -1 Chronicles 16:22; Psalms 105:15

60

Friend there is nothing new under the sun, you must be loathed like Christ was, so gird your loins together and fight.

CHAPTER 5

THE FIRE OF THE ENEMY

"The thief cometh not, but for to steal, and to kill, and to destroy..."
-        John 10:10

All that glitters is not gold.

Not every fire is intended to help you. God loves us, and because He does, He deliberately allows us to go through some very rough patches at times in order that He might bring out the best in us. Like fire applied to gold or to silver, it is meant to melt us so that the impurities in our lives can be conscientiously extracted. If it is applied for too long, the gold can lose some of its enviable qualities or be destroyed completely. If it is applied too little, it will simply not achieve what it was intended to achieve. As a matter of fact, yes, it can destroy the properties of the element as well, making it useless. Fire simply has to be applied just right.

We do not need to overstate the power or ability of the devil, but we do not need to understate it either. He is no stronger than we permit him because all power in heaven and on earth is given to Jesus

---

(Matthew 28:18), and hence us by inference (1 Corinthians 3:21). But the devil is crafty beyond words, considering all the experience he has had from manipulating mankind since Adam and Eve in the Garden of Eden way back when. And if there is one quality that defines him above all else, it is malice. Hate. The wanton obsession to defile and desecrate all that is precious to God. It is what drives and motivates him (Revelations 12) ...he knows he has been defeated and cast out of heaven; his place is no longer there (Revelations 12:8). So he is mad at man and wants to take as much of man down with him as he can.

"...Woe to the inhabiters of the earth and of the sea! For the devil is come down unto you, having great wrath, because he

*knoweth that he hath but a
shorttime.*" -Revelations 12:12b

A lot of people appear not to understand this –
it is why so many fall so easily to some of the
silliest distractions.

Let me put it this way: the devil does not care
if you are rich or poor – it means *nothing* to
him. He is the prince of this world. (John
12:31; 14:30), and all of the kingdoms of this
world have been his for quite a long time
(Matthew 4:8-9). He cares however, if you
have a relationship with God or not, and if that
relationship is growing... or not. He offered
Jesus the kingdoms of the world if Jesus
would bow down and worship him.

My heart chills as I try to imagine how many
people in the world today we hold in high
regard because they are wealthy and appear to
have the kingdoms of the world in their grasp.
I wonder how many of them succumbed to
that same devious enticement by Satan.
Gifted, yes. Successful, apparently. Popular,
well known and widely regarded, but firmly
belonging to the prince of this world because
they bowed. I imagine then how many of us
look up to these same people and envy them,

wanting the very same things that they have, hardly even bothering to ask ourselves: how did they get that rich that fast?

What the devil wants is your soul. You. For this, he will do just about anything – anything he is permitted to do by God, or by you, courtesy of your own ignorance or inattentiveness to treasured detail. He will offer you wealth if he thinks wealth will keep you away from Jesus. He will offer you food if he finds that you are a slave to your belly. And he will strike you with disease, deficiency, or death, if he can determine that any of these things will make you "curse God and die" (Job1&2).

He batters our flesh

The fires we are exposed to mostly affect our flesh for the purpose of bringing it under subjection to the things of the spirit. Our flesh is so susceptible to lusts – carnal desires – which have the powerful tendency to draw our attention away from things of the Spirit. God is a Spirit, you see; and they that worship Him must do so in spirit and in truth (John 4:24). Because we are so predisposed to feeding our flesh, we may never become sensitive to spiritual things until our flesh is broken down so that it no longer can get in the way.

65

One of the devil's most persistent weapons – and I daresay, about his most effective – is to consistently batter the flesh with desires, lusts, which invade the senses and keep the individual distracted from the true things that matter, which are the things of the spirit. Beautiful women, profligate parties and entertainment, fast and beautiful cars, money to the heart's content…, name it.

There's a reason why Jesus expressly states that it is easier for a camel to pass through the eye of a needle than for a rich man to enter into heaven (Matthew 19:24). He illustrates this with the rich young ruler who wanted to make heaven but had trouble letting go of the many lovely things that he had been able to amass through the course of his young but affluent life (Matthew 19:16-26). Keeping the law was relatively easy for him. Don't steal, don't kill, don't lie, do the Sabbath… When time came to become uncomfortable for the purpose of pleasing God, he simply couldn't do it.

Just as easily as he can distract someone by delivering ample supplies of these lusts, the devil can explore the possibly of depriving the same person or someone else of them if he believes it will serve his purpose. This is precisely what he did to Job, having obtained permission from God. The devil took his oxen, sheep, camels, his children, and eventually even his health, so much so his distraught wife urged him to curse God and die (Job chapters 1&2). Satan was very explicit too, about why he was doing this:

> *"Then Satan answered the LORD, and said, Doth Job fear the LORD for nought? Hast thou not made an hedge about him, and about his house, and about all he had on every side? Thou hast blessed the work of his hands, and his substance is increased in the land. But put forth thine hand now, and touch all that he hath, and he will curse thee to thy face."*

-       Job 1:9-11

Bear in mind, a bunch of thousand years later when Satan finally had the opportunity to put Jesus through the mill, his approach was the precise opposite: he offered Jesus all the kingdoms of the world!

In English, the devil does not care if you are rich or poor – all he cares about is if you have relationship with God, and if that relationship is in great shape or not. He will give anyone as much abundance as they can't handle if he can use that to turn their hearts away from God; and if he thinks that that is not working, he will do the reverse and take from them everything that they have if it will make them curse God and die.

This is why the Bible says:

> *"If any man come to me, and hate not his father, and mother, and wife, and children, and brethren, and sisters, yea, and his own life also, he cannot be my disciple. And whosoever doth not bear his cross, and come after me, cannot be my disciple...*
> *"So likewise, whosoever he be of you that forsaketh not all that he hath, he cannot be my disciple."*
> -   Luke 14:26-33

He can offer you a job as President of the United States if it will stop you from becoming the preacher that God wants you to

68

be. He will offer the most beautiful woman you have ever seen to marry if it will keep you from marrying the right woman who will help fulfil your God-ordained purpose as a classroom teacher. He will arrange for you to get a political assignment that will take you away from your family and from the place that God has placed you. He can arrange for you to be stuck in a church where there is no spiritual growth to speak of; or have your favorite television show come up at the precise time you are supposed to go out for evangelism. He has even been known to orchestrate an ordination as a pastor for someone who is meant to be out on the streets as an apostle.

This is the fire of the devil: it is intended to steal, kill, and destroy your time, your family, your hopes and aspirations, your purpose in Christ, your peace and joy, and eventually your very life and soul. Sometimes it can look so good that you don't want to walk away from it... like a gilded prison with the doors wide open. You are free to walk right out, but the bed is so cozy that you are having second thoughts because... ooh, because it feels *soo gooood*.

And if the luxuries do not work, he will offer affliction. Pain, suffering, loss. A job; an

69

accident; an injury; castigation from friends and family; ostracizing by those you really want to be part of; rejection; persecution; death of a loved one – *or many*; failure; the threat of death; poverty and penury; whatever he can muster, he will try if it will make you just take your gaze for one moment away from God and His divine plan for you.

We have to be able to turn a blind eye on the things that are in this world if we are hoping to walk with God and be effective at it. These things – these luxuries – are given for our convenience, yes, but they are never meant to take the place of God in our lives. The instant they start to become more important to us than the will and word of God, they have become idols and they have to go. If they stay, Holy Spirit quietly departs, not willing to contend with our free will. But the consequence of this is that we gradually begin to die because the devil would have achieved his primary purpose: our separation from God.

Some of the devil's fire against Moses was through the actions of Pharaoh. There was sentence of death issued before he was born, actuated in the royal command to have all Hebrew males murdered at birth. There was the identity crisis, perpetuated by the years lived in the palace as a Prince of Egypt, during which time the conflicted Moses wondered if he should suffer among his Hebrew brethren as a slave waiting to be exposed. There was the death sentence resurfaced, after Moses had acted presumptuously and slain one of Pharaoh's lieutenants.

Moses further endured fire as a fugitive in the scorching desert running from the law, and as a forgotten man in the wilderness, tending the sheep of his father-in-law, nowhere near the primary purpose for which he had been born. And finally, even after God had called him and given Moses his assignment, the fire continued through rejection from the people who ought to applaud him, the very ones who he was working to save.

Some of the most striking and impactful passages I have ever read are those of Moses interceding for the Israelites in the wilderness, even at times when they threatened to kill him. At one point he asked God to strike his name out of the His Book rather than exact wrath and vengeance upon the Israelites for making a graven idol (Exodus 32:32). At another point Moses and Aaron fell before the tabernacle to plead for the people when they murmured against him after the death of Korah, Dathan, and Abiram, to plead with the Lord not to destroy them.

These were the people he was working to save and they were turning on him. It got so bad at one point that Moses was eventually angered enough that he disobeyed God. This paints a picture of how longsuffering Moses had to have been to lead this people for 40 years. But all of it was fire – fire from the enemy, purposed to destroy him, to cut short the calling of God in his life. And it could only have been the marvelous glory of God that He could take all that pain and turn it around for the attainment of His divine purpose.

Joseph, another man who had undergone the fire of affliction said it best when he proclaimed to his brothers:

> *"But as for you, ye thought evil against me but God meant it unto good, to bring to pass, as it is this day, to save much people alive."* - Genesis 50:20

72

Only someone whom God has put through the mill and who has come out refined on the other side could have made such a statement. God uses the pain and the pleasure alike – everything that has ever happened to us, or ever will, can be employed by our Father in heaven toward achieving His grand purpose, but only those who end up being refined by it will be able to see it. Those who fail by succumbing to the lusts and other distractions often end up being sad and depressed, regularly blaming others for the mishaps that they experienced and for their failures as a result. In short, they never attain their divine calling.

The fire of the enemy is malicious, and at its height it can feel as though your life is at an end, like everything you've ever worked for or aspired to is simply over and done with. But even though it might hurt, if you are calm enough you will find that the worst of the torment lies in

your thinking – the things that
are in your mind.

———————————

Jesus put it this way:
> *"Not that which goeth into the*
> *mouth defileth a man; but that*
> *which cometh out of the*
> *mouth, this defileth a man."*
> -   Matthew 15:11

There are many things which happen to different people all the time, however the true value of who they are lies in what is in their hearts, their thoughts, which tend to come out when the fire is applied. As with silver exposed to flames, the dross quickly comes to the surface as the metal is liquefied so that the silversmith can remove the garbage and then reapply the fire until there is no more dross.

The torment for some of the unfortunate things which happen to us lie in the thoughts that we permit in our hearts and minds. We can for instance choose to stay sad and depressed, rerunning the unpleasant event over and over in our minds until it breaks out into something as nasty as bipolar disorder; or we might even try to suppress it, pretend it's not there, until

74

one day we break out and hurt someone close to us.

These are the things that come of our mouths when the fires are applied – they come from the abundance of our hearts and they influence the things we do and the things that further happen to us.

> *"A good man out of the treasure of his heart bringeth forth that which is good; and an evil man out of the evil treasure of his heart bringeth forth that which is evil; for of the abundance of the heart the mouth speaketh."*
>
> Luke 6:45

You can afford to examine your own life more closely: what are the things that I do and say when things get uncomfortable? That is the real person that you are, and it is born out of your thought process – those things that you try to hide from everybody else. Do you get irritable? Do you lash out? Do you carefully plan and orchestrate your revenge, or do you genuinely reach out an olive branch of peace

75

and forgiveness, longing to mend that which is broken? You may be able to deceive everyone – yourself included – but you cannot get it past God.

You may be able to deceive everyone – yourself included – but you cannot get it past God. He sees what is in your heart, buried under vain efforts to conceal it such as anger management, relationship management, personality, or charisma.

But God looks in your heart and sees the real wickedness that is there. To be fair, it's not your fault – it's the fallen nature, the man of sin. But you have absolutely no control over him because you are a slave to sin; at least you *were* until Jesus found you.

To beat it, however, you have a role to play – that of submission to the Holy Spirit and obedience to the Word.

"Finally, brethren, whatsoever things are true, whatsoever

things are honest, whatsoever things are just, whatsoever things are pure, whatsoever thins are lovely, whatsoever things are of good report; if there be any virtue, and if there be any praise, think on these things."

-      Philippians 4:8

Chapter 6

God's Miracle of Preservation

God the El-Shaddai is such a wonder in all things and all areas of life. How could He have made provision for a way of escape for Moses, for Joseph for Adam and Eve or even the Apostles? How did He preserve and provide for Jesus and all His people in the Old and New Testament before even though the ferocious king and slave drivers were bent on killing and destroying all those people? His loving kindness is better than life in deed.

One thing we need to bear in mind as God's children is that through trials and temptations, through the pressures of life, he wants our needs met. No wonder the psalmist boldly declared that the Lord is his shepherd and he shall not want. It is also not much wander when in the Lord's Prayer we are instructed to ask God for our daily bread. John puts a head

78

to it when he declared that it is the will of God for us to prosper and be in health even as our souls prosper. We must be bold always to say and live on this revelation of God's word in whatever condition; whether we are in the pressure cooker or in the oven or right under the hell of a fire! God did not only provide for Moses, but he also preserved him through thick and thin. Sure, he is ready to do the same for you. Can you picture Joseph in prison or Gideon on his divine assignment. Mighty God had their backs and he sure has your back too.

There are some destinies that are screaming. Under fire but not consumed, because they are under the personal eye and protection of our heavenly Father. They cannot be killed.

Father may permit the devil to fire some of his deadliest arrows at us, but still the decree concerning us is: "You cannot kill this one."

Even before Moses arrived with a sentence of death hanging over his head, there were the midwives in Goshen charged by the Pharaoh to see to it that no male Hebrew child was left

79

alive at birth, but these women made a plan to disobey the Pharaoh's edict. It was because, even unbeknownst to them, there was a child coming, and they could not break the neck of that child. God rewarded them for preserving the lives of the Hebrew infants.

Nobody can break your neck, because before you started out God knew you were coming. He has prepared you for an assignment even before you were formed in your mother's womb (Jeremiah 1:5; Romans 8:29-30).

However, Moses was born despite the plans of the devil. By the time he was born the decree had been announced – every Jewish boy child was now illegal and was to be killed. Many mothers and fathers lost their babies this way, but when Moses' parents birthed him, they were able to perceive and see that he was a proper child, a child of destiny; and they said, no, no, this one cannot be killed. We are going to protect him and risk our lives doing so.

You want to believe that also about yourself – there are some people who are coming your way who are going to risk their lives for your great destiny to be fulfilled, because for

God... *you're worth it.* And as a prophet of God I summon them to come forth today.

ONE DOOR CLOSES BUT OTHERS WILL OPEN

Amram and Jochebed kept their boy illegally for three months until their ability to keep it up was exhausted. Now there was nothing more. Have you ever had such a report? We've done all we could; this is as far as we go. We are sorry, we enjoyed it while it lasted, but this is the end of the road. We can't do anything more.

Have your parents ever thrown you out of the house? Has your spouse ever walked out on you? Have you ever been given the sack just when you thought you could no longer be stopped? Have you ever been diagnosed with a debilitating terminal disease just when you thought life was just beginning? Or has your own best friend ever stabbed you in the back and taken a job that was intended for you? There are all kinds of ways people can decide that they have come far enough with you in this life and it was time to cut you lose.

"What can we do for him?" Moses' frustrated

81

and exhausted parents were despondent. "Let's send him to the crocodiles," they decided. They then prepared an ark with leaves in a basket, and put his last meal by his side and dropped him in the water of the River Nile, a river infested with crocodiles.
The Bible says,

"When my mother and my father forsake me then the Lord will take me up"

Psalms 27:10), and that was exactly what happened – God stepped into the situation and orchestrated it to its next phase.

It's not over. When man says it's over, it is only just the beginning with God. When the same people who used to hold it down for you suddenly turn and say "We're down and out; we've done all we can; this time we walk," guess what? Immediately you take the first step to walk on your own, God steps up and takes charge. See, God just wants you to know without an iota of a doubt that you could never have done any of it without His help, simply to prove that there is no other God in your life because He *is* a jealous God. He's the one who has the blueprint of your life. He saw you and

82

formed you. He called you forth and sent you forth. Now He will not deny His name in your life, especially not now with your Destiny Under Fire.

FLOATING BETWEEN CROCODILES AND SURVIVING IT

So we have Moses sailing on the waters of Nile, hungry crocodiles swimming right past him, ready to break their fast. Sure, the crocodiles saw him. It's just that they saw the angels too – the ones who were on guard over that little floating basket. The crocodiles wisely decided that their lives weren't worth the little meal that was floating by.

I pray that the angels in charge of protecting your destiny will rise up right now and banish every hovering crocodile seeking to consume your destiny, in the Name of Jesus. The hour has come. Every 'croc' *'croc-ing'* their eyes and licking their tongues at you or me, are commanded to back off right now. Invisible angels begin to declare: "Back off, back off, back off, back off, back off, not this one," just as they did to protect Moses.

And in the same vein, another angel went

83

ahead and whispered into the ear of the princess in the palace, "What are you still doing in bed? Its daybreak. Take your maidens, get on out to the Nile for your regular shower. You *want* to be at a specific location where I have an assignment especially tailored for you."

PROPHETIC HELPING HANDS IN DESTINY

When you are a child of destiny, God always sets up appointments for you. If you miss one, He sets up another. If you miss five, He re-routes you another still. That's where God differs from man. Man tell you, an opportunity once missed can never be regained. Whereas this may make a lot of common sense, God cares enough about you to continue creating opportunities every step of the way. When you worry about missing this or that, lamenting over what may have happened or failed to happen ten years ago, God is actually already at work rerouting your life to be made perfect unto Him. Why, an ordinary Lincoln Navigator can reroute you… You think the Divine Navigator cannot? If you miss one, he reroutes. You miss another, He reroutes. You miss another, He reroutes.

It's not over until you win.

You should say this quick and simple prayer:

Every Princess or prince with a new assignment over my life, why are you sleeping over my destiny? Stir up yourself, rise up, I summon you, come by my side right now and do the work of God in my life.

Just imagine how the princess walked into the scene. She came, and as she came by there was the cry of a baby. Babies cry, but I bet this one was a screaming one yelling out a cry for destiny. And the same way God cannot ignore your screaming destiny, men cannot ignore it either – nor could the princess ignore Moses'. You may be under fire, but men cannot ignore you. Even your season cannot ignore you any longer. This nation cannot ignore you;

The cry of the infant penetrated this gentile woman's consciousness and registered a coded message. When she would have said "oh, that's a Jewish baby; I'll get the guards to kill him," she found herself naming a little infant boy whom she knew that her father wanted dead!

The baby was brought to the princess and he

flashed her that timeless and priceless smile: "I am the one that you've been waiting for; your divine assignment; the one to give meaning to your meaninglessness and purpose to your purposelessness."

You know, some people have money but their money is meaningless and purposeless until they meet you. The earth is the Lord's and the fullness thereof… He is thence the one who decides what goes where, why, and for whom. People who believe that they have properties cannot find purpose to all of it because they are only caretakers managing them until you come in with an edict and assignment from the Holy One. And so they line up and begin to fall for you in pleasant places simply because Father has said, it is time.

DIVINE DRAMA

Suddenly, the princess of Egypt had a sense of value now and purpose now. She could not just be called upon at any time for royal frivolities anymore; she could respond with "I am busy; I have a baby to take care of." Prior to then she was no more than a female with a tiara on her head, beautiful and shaking her waist with each step, but living a totally pointless life. But where she would wake up in the mornings, bathe herself in scented perfumes, and hang around with doting servants all day doing nothing before, now she had become a nursing mother with a purpose – a mother looking to employ some Hebrew woman with anointed breast milk to cater to a special baby, her mind burdened with resolve: "Who can I get?"

Somebody said, "I know of a woman; and, the princess said, "Go and call her."
So they summon the boy's mother and they had a conversation:
"Woman I hear that you have ability to take care of this child of destiny. Name your salary. Have you got some Jewish breast milk?"
"Yes ma'am."
"Is the milk still flowing?"
"Very fresh."
"Alright, what's your price?"
And Jochebed dictated the price she would be paid to breastfeed her own child.

You cannot tell me God is dead. I'm alive today because He woke me up this morning. I beg you in the name of Jesus, on my knees, stop putting my God on the same scale as the devil. God has no fight with the devil. He has finished with all of that a bunch of thousand years ago. He whipped him good, and this time, He sends the devil to you for target practice.

Same boy they did not want, same boy they created a decree of death for, the devil went to sleep and the boy had a harness built for him in the palace with soldiers to take care of him, while his own mother on a paycheck from the treasury suckled him.

O, for many years I functioned as an illegal alien in the United States of America. But I know I carry some anointing – Destiny under fire – and I would travel and go preach around the country. Sometimes I had to fly, I would go to the airport to catch a flight, and I would fly without a hitch. Some people have done similar things, but when you carry that title of 'illegal alien' in America, you run from the airport because you don't need the authorities getting on your case. But here I was, running to the airport – not once, but repeatedly.

"Where are you going?"
"A meeting in Phoenix (or in Dallas

perhaps)."

"OK, may I have your license?"

"Hmmm...No license...Will you take a debit card?"

"Are you crazy? Step aside".

"Alright, sir."

I soon determined that I was being asked to "step aside" quite often(too many times) and I purposed that I would always go to the airport three hours before the flight so that they would have enough time to exhaust themselves. When eventually they got around to me, they would always ask the inevitable question: "Who are you?"

My usual response: "I am a servant of the Living God. I have an assignment to go and bless some people somewhere."

"OK, I pray that your God will do it. Go on the flight. Have a nice flight." That is how it has been, and I have relished every moment of it.

Listen. Every time the devil comes to you, he creates an opportunity for praise for God. Every single time I got past airport security. My hands would go up in the air and the words would come spilling from my heart right out

my mouth:
"Who is the Lord besides our God? Who is the Rock besides our God? My fortress and my shield, the power of deliverance is his, the one who trusts in the King. He trains my hands to war, and leads me in His triumph forever, praise His name forever more."
Yes, I know how to float between the crocodiles – I have lived that life for so long it has become second-nature to me now – being victorious. And when the crocs come at me now I say hold off, hold off, hold off, I'm destiny under fire.

In the palace, Pharaoh was practically paying for the life and growth of the same child he had tried so hard to murder. Under his very roof, Moses grew, until finally they paid off his mother's final salary and let her go. You want to be careful how you treat people of destiny when they are in your care because it is a measure of the kind of regard you have for God. When Moses left the care of his mother, the incoming salaries from the princess dried up, same as the Ark of the Covenant leaving the home of Obed-Edom; or Elijah leaving the home of the Widow of Zarephat. The blessings didn't evaporate or anything, but the provision that came with the anointed person stopped. A person of destiny may come to you looking stranded. You want to take them in and give them the best care that you can manage. That shows God how much you regard Him, and He tends to bring a blessing to you because of it – you *know* that my Father will never owe anybody.

God gave my wife and myself a warning in May of 1981 that I will not soon forget.
"I am going to send you many people," He said. "When they get to you they will be stranded. Tell your wife to wash their feet because they are the same people I will use to help you."

They came, and we welcomed them. Before we left Nigeria, more than two hundred and seventy people had passed through our home and we were blessed to be a blessing unto them. In those days my house was simply an open thoroughfare, and I was glad to be a tool in use for the divine purpose of God.

Hallelujah.
I drove for six years once, without a driver's

license. *Destiny under fire.*
One day, after I was I done preaching in one of the Boroughs, my phone rang and I picked it. Almost immediately after, I heard that short beep of police sirens right behind my car and I literally froze.

"Ok Baba, where's my flight back to Nigeria?"
The officer drove up and around me, then said, "Wind down the glass."

I did, totally expecting to hear something like "May I see your license and registration, please?" Not a question, but a statement for cold hard reality. Instead the man pointed his police finger in my face and said, "Sir, hang up that phone and go home. Good night!"

I said a hasty and relieved "Yes sir, good night," and got myself out of there before he changed his mind.

Destiny under Fire!
One other day there was a revival, a great one that lasted eight straight days. At the end of the event, I was drunk in my head, saying, "Let me go pick the man of God from the hotel and take him to a restaurant."

Somehow I drove past the hotel and had to turn the car back around to return to pick up this pleasant man – a wonderful Bishop –and we just sat in the car. I wanted to drive him right up to the buffet where he would load up, but again I mistakenly took another wrong turn and ended up staring several State Troopers on the way in the middle of traffic. More than seven of these officers were with their vehicles.

Something had to have gone wrong. They had barricaded the road and seemed to be in no hurry to vacate. I got a bit worried. Would I still be able to just drive past? I was thinking, and then I stopped in the middle of the road they got angry. One of them came to the front and said "Pull up that car! Park it aside!" My wife began to speak, *"Supernatural 911, Express Department of heaven, send help. There's destiny here under fire."*

"Your license and your registration."
I wanted to say I did not have any, but before the words got out of my mouth the Holy Spirit said, "You have."

I said, "Hello Officer," at the same time as I

was talking to the Holy Spirit asking Him, "What do you mean 'I have'?"

He said, "you have your old Nigerian driver's license inside your wallet, pull it out."
"How are you Officer? Everything going well today?" I pulled out the Nigerian driver's license and flashed it. The man didn't even look at the date on the thing.

He said, "You are from Nigeria? Wonderful. And you can drive in America? Wonderful. Do you drive on the left side or right in Nigeria? You know what? Wonderful. Please be safe. Drive safely."

I said, "Thank you, Officer," and we were on our way
I am Destiny Under Fire!

VISIONS AND TROUBLE
Dare to dream or nurture a Vision bigger than yourself and it won't be long before all hell break-loose. The devil don't mind you living your entire life as an ordinary fellow with no appetite for big dreams; but as soon as you step of the crowds, trouble comes!

The first forty years in the palace, Moses was a prince of Egypt; educated in the best Egyptian schools by the best Egyptian tutors. The man rated better than everybody his equal. Then he started having dreams of trouble. Every day he would dream, seeing himself among slaves. What devilry was this? He was prince! I imagine Moses finally must have gone to his mother and said, "Mom, I don't understand. How come every time I dream I see myself as an illegal alien?"

Mama would have said, "My dear son, there are secrets of the secret, and the secret of the secret is a secret."

"Mama, can you talk to me?"
"My son, you are destiny under fire. You were conceived in a Jewish womb. As a matter of fact, you sucked a Jewish breast."
"So, I am not a prince?"
"O sure, you are a prince of Egy…I mean of God."

Identity Crisis.
So many people are going through all kinds of identity crises today. People look at you and

say you are confused. No, you are not confused; you are a destiny under fire.

Moses finally came to a settled position, a place where it all seemed *past* and done with. Then the heavens opened and he began to see visions of God.

You can never fully identify who you are until you begin to see what God says of you. He formed you after all; He designed your parts, carefully crafted your temperament, and orchestrated the events in your life for a special purpose that was always dear to Him. Even when the enemy thought they had a hold on you, God was watching, like a refiner at a refiner's fire (Malachi 3:2-3), making sure that the fire doesn't consume you, but rather that it perfects you.

Your situation cannot define you appropriately – only God can. Men and women looking at you cannot define you – hey, they have their own fiery paths to walk. Your struggle cannot define you either, because they are not an end, they are a means. What you might call a failure really is a preparation for a certain success, which is why it also cannot define you. What defines you is what God made you to be, what He says about you.

You are destiny under fire.
Finally, heaven downloaded Moses' blueprint unto Him:
Boy, before you were born, there was a sentence of death, but I caused you to escape. It was Me; not your mother or father. When your mother and father dropped you off at the Nile, I it was who picked you up from among the crocodiles, shutting their mouths by my angels. They killed others but they would never be able to kill you because you are destiny under fire. All that time you enjoyed the treasures of Egypt, I assigned them to you. I made kings and princes your nursing mothers to prepare you. I brought you to a land that you did not know. I arranged for you to sleep in beds you never saw before. You ate food until you ran from it and started doing your weight loss program. *I* the Lord was the one who has always been behind the scenes for your life. Even while you twisted your nose and said, "I know, I know, I know," I knew where you were coming from. I brought

97

you from there, and none other. *Because you are a destiny under fire.*
You think this palace is something? Wait until I show you visions of the palace of heaven.

The Lord took him in visions and showed him the glory of heaven, so that he declared that he would rather identify with the reproach of Christ than to dwell in Egypt to enjoy the treasures of sin for a season (Hebrews 11:23-38).

THIS IS YOUR MOMENT TO STEP OUT
"I'm going to step out," he said. "because I am *Destiny Under Fire*." So Moses went out to check on his brethren. To him they were no more slaves, but 'brethren'.

You want to remember this going forward all the days of your life: the mark of true blessing running through your veins is to be able to look at the rejected and see value where no one else did, to see beauty where others perceived ugliness, and to not be able to walk past broken humanity as if they don't count unless and until you are able to do something about it. This is what Christ meant in Matthew 22, speaking about separating the entire world into goats and sheep, and letting the sheep go in while the goat stayed out – no, *while they went to hell!*

Moses went and saw his brethren suffering. And when he saw a well-fed, chested, and muscular Egyptian unjustly beating a Hebrew slave, something inside him snapped.

Leaning on your own understanding is a reckless endeavor which can lead you to take dangerous steps.

Nothing permits you to calculate on God, which rather tends to lead one down the path of self-destruction, and by the time you realize what you've done… - Bam! Moses had slain the Egyptian to save the Hebrew guy.

Oh wow, that's an Egyptian Prince killing one of his own people.

Rejection and Mistaken Identity.

Even those he was called to save did not know or acknowledge him, setting up a background for rejection. This is something we want to forever bear in mind: any man or woman of destiny under fire will go through the gates of rejection at some point, either self-orchestrated or externally manipulated. Nobody wants to be rejected, but *except a grain of wheat fall to the ground and die, it abideth alone,* and rejection is a significant part of the falling to the ground and dying in God's book. Somehow or the other, He Himself lets these things happen!

Next day, Moses wanted to do the right thing, saving his own brethren from fighting each other. Then one of those big, lousy, foul-mouthed Hebrew brethren spoke up:
"Hah. You want to kill me like you killed the Egyptian yesterday? Who made you ruler and judge over us?" The silly fellow blew the whistle on Moses, and suddenly destiny under fire was on the run again. Funny thing is, this thing really isn't that strange actually. Remember Joseph getting sold into slavery by his own brothers? Remember David being driven into the wilderness by Saul? Remember Jesus bearing that heavy cross on the lonely road to Calvary? It's not that farfetched at all to find the very same people you are trying to help turn around and set you up for the fall. It's human nature; but there's no getting around the fact that it is one of the most

100

painful experiences in destiny under fire: betrayal.

No, not betrayal by enemies – you expect that; you're prepared subconsciously for it. But betrayal by those who are supposed to love and nurture you, those you are supposed to lean on, the same ones you expect much from… that cuts *deep*. You expect such a person to give you their shoulder but they move away and let you collapse. They should lend that helping hand, but instead they are the ones wondering why you are not dead. They would even check in on you after a while – not to offer support, you see, to learn what in the world could be holding you together.

We thought you'd be totally frustrated by now.
We honestly thought there was no way on earth you could have made it through that.
Frankly, we thought you would be already dead.

But you can't die, sir. You're destiny under fire! You may look dead, but you can't die. Because you haven't quite done your assignment just yet. It doesn't matter what the enemy hits you with, you are not going to die until you have fulfilled the assignment for which you were born.

There was a man of destiny under fire: an old man. He thought he had done everything in his life that needed to be done, and so he was praying, "God I have done everything. All my mates and colleagues are gone. Why am I still here? I'd like to die and go already." But God had a whole different story of him to tell, and God said to him, "Hmm-hmm, Mr. Simeon. You aren't quite done yet. Until you see the Messiah in the flesh, no you are not going to die." So everybody was there, he was waiting —

And so he waited…
"*I'm waiting for my day to join the ranks…*"
and one day, just like any other, a young man and woman brought in an infant child to the temple for the traditional ceremonials, and as Old Man Simeon set about his duties, Holy Spirit spoke the long awaited words to him: "Ah-ah, this is the Messiah." It was a day of appointment.

"This is the day that I have waited for? Are you kidding me? This is the Messiah lying in my arms right now? Wow. Mine eyes have seen the salvation of the Lord, prepared before the face of all the people. Light to the gentiles and glory of Israel. Now let thy servant depart in peace" (Luke 2:25-35).

Yes, I know you are destiny under fire. Yes, I know you have seen more than a few rough days in your time – maybe even more so than anyone else that you know. Yes, you are probably feeling like Elijah that said: "*...It is enough; now, O Lord, take away my life; for I am not better than my fathers...*" (1 Kings 19:4-14). I'm excited to announce to you, you are going to see your day. Yes, y*ou are!* Because you are destiny under fire.

TROUBLE ALWAYS SEEM TO TRAIL SOME FOLKS

Moses secret was blown here. With that one act of betrayal he was reduced from prince-hood to fugitive status, wanted dead or alive. Suddenly that sentence of death he had escaped as an innocent infant was upon him again, just like some people can't seem to escape problems and circumstances from their past. They had to live with it in their country, but they got the visa and came over to the United States, and the silly thing is just waiting right here for them to arrive.

103

Here's the really interesting thing: it doesn't change anything in God's book. You *are* destiny under fire!

Moses was a real illegal alien now – why, that's what he named his son: *"because he said I've been a stranger in a strange land,"* undocumented, unsanctioned, and unknown. The real thing and chief of them. But all was not yet lost. The man still had some skills – primarily the passion and ability to fight for justice. And even though he had been betrayed, the skills and attributes he had been endowed with did not leave him. Those were still going to go along with him whichever way he was led.

One of the greatest disasters that can happen to anyone is if they let their circumstances reconfigure them. If you let people's betrayal rearrange you, if you let those unfortunate circumstances change your person or your passion, or you let them shift your gaze away from Jesus, which would be a terrible shame. I'm going to say it again: you cannot let the circumstance of life turn you into somebody that you are not. Frankly that is what I would term as you throwing away your own destiny.

Moses was still fighting for justice, but he couldn't do it there anymore. It was his passion for justice that got him in trouble, but that did not mean that he needed to quit now. A pregnant woman wants to have her baby; she can't quit then on the night before her delivery only because she has to deal with labour pains. She has to push through the pain and have that baby, otherwise the baby could die and she could very well lose her own life also.

There's a reason why Americans say that you don't change horses mid-stream. Jesus Himself put it this way: "...*No man having put his hand on the plough, and looking back, is fit for the kingdom of God.*" (Luke 9:62)

God don't appreciate second thoughts, buyer's remorse, or any other such thing. He wants you to make up your mind and stick with it. That's what faith is, and that's what moves the hand of God.

> *"If any of you lack wisdom, let him ask of God, that giveth to all men liberally, and upbraideth not; and it shall be given him. But let him ask in*

faith, nothing wavering. For
he that wavereth is like a wave
of the sea driven with the wind
and tossed. For let not that
man think that he shall receive
any thing of the Lord."
-        James 1:5-7

If you are going to walk with God, you have to be decisive. You don't change your mind or change your track just because things got nasty on the way. They *will* get nasty at some point. When they do, God sticks with you and expects nothing less from you. If you stay the course and don't try to change your personality because things have gotten unpleasant for you on the way, a new dawn will inevitably arise and you will be that much better for it.

GOD FOCUSES THE BEST IN THE WORST MOMENT

The passionate fight for justice which was burning in Moses was surely still going to give him a new deal. Soon on the far side of the desert, he found himself fighting to protect the virtue and rights of ladies he did not know anything about. How was he to know that one of them was going to be his new partner for the assignment that was to be his life? The ladies reported to their father, and the old man come out with, "What are you talking about? I am a priest and I have been dreaming about that man. Bring him in."

"Hey boy. Have a good meal. You look as though you are desert-tutored. I can see the prince in you even though the desert has rearranged you."

Can *you* see the prince in people even when the desert has rearranged them? Can you honor the prince in people who have been battered by the desert? Do you respect the prince or princess in you even when you have been battered by the desert?

LITTLE THINGS LEADS TO BIG MOMENTS

They gave him food, and he said, "Boy, do you need an assignment? There is a job opening here, and I need a pastor for my sheep and my goats."

"That would be a nice job," replies this sun-burnt stranger who had never done any real work in his entire life… but he didn't think he was too big for it. Prince or not, life needed to move on and he needed to take this bull by the horn. See, if you are too big for small things then you are not really big on the inside, and nobody serious is going to think you are big enough for the big things either. This is a serious lesson that we all need to learn, and one that Jesus Himself made clear while He walked the earth:

> *"He that is faithful in that which is least is faithful also in much: and he that is unjust in the least is unjust also in much. If therefore ye have not been faithful in the unrighteous mammon, who will commit to your trust the true riches? And if ye have not been faithful in that which is another man's, who shall give you that which is your own?"*
> -   Luke 16:10-12

God is not in the business of rewarding slothfulness with promotion. If there's something big on the horizon for you, God is in the habit of putting little things in the way for you to overcome in order to prepare you for the big deal when it hits. As such, you can't have your head so high up in the sky that you refuse to lower yourself to do the menial assignments. If you do, you could just be delaying the big reward God has intended for you.

O, God is patient. He can wait until you get your act together. *You are the one who is in a hurry and bound by time; He isn't.* You are the one who needs to get down and do the dirty. Like Paul said, forget the things that are past and press toward the mark of the prize of the high calling (Philippians 3:13-14), so that you can show yourself worthy of that which is still coming. Moses certainly did.

I once pastored a church in Atlanta where I found that a number of people couldn't pay their cell phone bills at one point.
I called to a sister and said, "Sister, why don't you try CNA,"

She said "No, I can't wash anybody's butt."
Funny, yet every month end we wash the butt of her cell phones with our church offerings.

109

That's not dignity. You can do all things through Christ who strengthens you. And it is not what you are doing that defines who you are; if you are really secure on the inside you can do almost *anything*. Besides, it's just for the season; a bus stop is not your destination. It just happens to be someplace you have to pass through in order to get to where you are going.

Moses took this job, and the man said, "You know what? You see my daughter out there? What do you think about her?"

The boy said, "Sir, she's a lovely lady, sir."
"Ok, we have a deal. You go say hello to her and both of you can go on off into the wilderness for a little chat."

By the time they returned, Moses was married to this woman he had not known, however, she was a woman whom God had prepared in that season to comfort and nurture this man of destiny.

MIRACLES OF PRESERVATION
You should know that there are certain people in your wilderness moment who show up after all the big names, and those you knew and

were comfortable with have vanished. These are people you did not know and you totally did not plan for them, but God planned and prepared them for you, and sent them ahead so that they can comfort you in that moment when everyone else thinks you are pretty much done for. It is because you are destiny under fire, and you need the right hands, the right kind of touch, so that the fire does not destroy you when you are in it.

Jethro and his family took care of Moses. They brought him into their home and gave him a sense of value that would have been challenged by the jarring transformation from royalty to wilderness. All of a sudden Moses felt like a married man *because he was*. And this married man began to have children. One, two... life was getting good. He had become Assistant Pastor to his father-in-law's church of goats and chicken.

The Bible tells us in Matthew 11:12 that "*and from the days of John the Baptist until now the kingdom of heaven suffereth violence and the violent taketh it by force*" You must take your destiny by force because your destiny is under violent harassment of hell. Hell has a conspiracy to abort your destiny. And this is the disaster in church. Too often we focus on the toys and abandon the destiny. Looking for miracles, we lose sight of our destiny and inheritance. The original deal, that's what you want. Church will bring you some miracles, but there is yet a destiny that must be fulfilled.

It is a miracle for a man under rejection from everything he used to know to suddenly find a new home in the desert, yes, but that is a far cry from destiny. It is a miracle that he now has a job – Assistant Pastor of Jethro's flock; but that was not his destiny. It most certainly *is* a miracle that Moses got a lady to look after him – a stranded man without so much as a job or even a title to his name.

The man this lady married was no more than her father's goat and chickens' overseer, not even a citizen of the land. Just an illegal alien and a fugitive on the run. In spite of all that, Zephorah married this man who had a destiny, looking terrible as he did he was however a terrific man.

Seriously, to get a wife under those circumstances is really one big and undeniable miracle. And then babies. All of these miracles of encouragement were occurring in the life of this man who was supposed to be on the losing side of things. Even though they were not exactly his destiny, they were solace – growth – given him when he should have been broken. His destiny was still waiting, under fire, but waiting the meantime he was growing on so many other sides.

This is a lesson to many of us in this life who have become bitter and ungrateful for the little opportunities that present themselves when our lives are on the back-burner of ignominy while in backside of the desert. A phase of our lives when things aren't going the way we think they should go is a trying time when men are made or broken. As a result, we could become so bitter that we miss out on opportunities for solace to carry us through these. Moses had the presence of mind to accept a menial assignment and sit with it for 40 years; he had the good heart to love and permit himself to be loved when he was at his lowest ebb; and somehow he started to become fruitful again as the Lord continued to expand his coast in preparation for something that was inevitable.

Somebody popped a question when Moses came under rejection: *"who made you a ruler and a judge over us?"* Well, God was answering that question right now – the process of making him a ruler and a judge was in the wilderness among goats and chickens. One year. Two years. Three… All the way up to forty years, Moses was in a place of destiny under fire, until finally fire broke out from heaven because his time had come!

IT'S YOUR MOMENT, RIDE IT TO THE MAX!

He was always going to and coming back around the same place for forty years but that was about to change forever! The man Moses woke up that morning in the house of his father-in-law, broken perhaps but not done, without his own house, married but living with his in-laws, two boys growing up calling him Daddy. Moses woke up that day, and it all looked as though it was going to be another one dreary day in the same place, 40 years and counting. But on this day something was waiting that could no longer be denied because it was time.

Moses woke up that day…

"*My sweetheart*" he whispered to his darling Zipporah, and then got up with a goatly purposed: "Yeah goats, let's go. Come on into church. Chickens? Time to go!!"

That was when a fire broke out from heaven, and all of a sudden the man sees a bush is burning – not entirely unusual – only this time, *the bush is not being consumed by the flames*! Ok. Bush normally burn. But there is something about this bush. It's not consumed. The bush is burning but it's not consumed. He said

Oooh, new territory.

Sometimes we just need to realize that we are at the cusp of something entirely new and revolutionary, on a threshold where our destiny is about breaking forth. And in those moments we need to be able to take the right step toward it without fear. Call it curiosity; call it duty or responsibility; in that moment, you had better pray that you have the courage and presence of mind to step forward and embrace it so that you don't wait around for a few more years before it comes back around.

God said to Moses through that bush: "I have

heard the cry of my people."

Obviously, it was not about Moses himself that God spoke, but about the people to whom God was sending Moses. See, Moses was already destiny under fire, but being activated; but those to whom God was sending him still needed to be delivered not just from their physical bondage, but from the bondage of their minds. So that message you're getting, is really not about you at all; it's about your neighbor. It's about all those lost hungry souls out there that need deliverance. And you are the tool that the Lord has purposed to use to bring forth His glory.

"I have a job to do," the Lord was saying to Moses. "And you are the man for the job." "Hey, just wait up a little bit – I can't speak. I'm not eloquent". "Well, it doesn't matter," saith the Lord. "Whatever your disability is becomes my opportunity to show myself God in your life."So what, you don't have a green card? I will use you like that. You don't have a yellow card? I can use you like that. You lack an education; I've got it covered. Whatever is your disability, it has become my opportunity to get Myself the glory.

116

Do not sit down and moan when you are going through your oven experiences or through fire. You need to keep your focus for God will use what you have, and more so use the so called suffering and terrible experience to bring you into the limelight of your destiny.

Part 2

FROM THE REED
TO THE ROCK

Chapter 7

THE CALLED PETER

"For a just man falleth seven times, and riseth up again: but the wicked shall fall into mischief."
-        Proverbs 24:16

"The steps of a good man are ordered by the Lord: and he delighteth in his way. Though he fall, he shall not be utterly cast down: for the Lord upholdeth him with his hand."
-        Psalm 37:23-24

In life we fall and rise many times as we grow – it is as much a part of life as, say, breathing. Even when we seem to have grown, we are constantly developing and changing in many areas of our lives that may sometimes not be visible. This growth process can be painful on their own, but occasionally certain situations come around and we still stumble and fall. It is unfortunate that a lot of people take this as the end of life as they know it, and they begin to give up in their minds.

Isaiah 43:2 is so explicit as it says:
> **When you pass through the waters, I will be with you; and when you pass through the rivers, they will not sweep over you. When you walk through the fire, you will not be burned; the flames will not set you ablaze.**

When we go through fire, it is part of our growing process, and it is possible sometimes to stumble while inside that fire and find ourselves flat on our face. God doesn't expect us to give up in such an instance; He wants us to get up, dust ourselves off, and get right back on the horse, whatever we have to do –
> **because He has already made the grace available for it!** (2 Corinthians 9:8)

When my son was trying to walk he had many falls, though I honestly did not like it, I felt sorry for him but I could not help him. He was going to have to walk, I can't do his walking for him regardless of how much I loved him. So while I loved and cared for him, while I would occasionally offer a hand to pull him back up or guide his steps, I would still stand back and watch him try again and again until he finally found his footing and was able to stand and walk by himself. Of course, today we both look back and laugh at those days, grateful that they came because they had to. He's a better man for it now.

Such is life. You've been through it; I've been through it; and we will all still go through something again and again until we are all perfected in Christ. Even the seemingly most successful of men in the world today will tell you interesting tales of how they have fallen and risen many times and over. As a matter of fact very few businessmen get it right at the initial stage because they are still learning the ropes and do not yet know of certain business practices they should adopt and the ones they should avoid like a plague. So they make mistakes, some of them to the point of losing the entire business and having to start again.

Everyone at one point or the other pays a price for their success. Thomas Edison, the popular inventor, made several mistakes on the part to his inventions but he saw something that others did not see. He had a destiny to fulfill. And even though he had to be fronted with funds on occasion, he kept at it and today, *"The Wizard of Menlo Park"* is known through history as a businessman and America's greatest inventor.

I am personally a fan of Peter the Apostle and the story of his life from the day He met Jesus to the point of his death by upside-down crucifixion in Rome, circa AD 68. The man was a beautiful example of how God can take somebody ordinary, put him through the mill and fire, carry him through stumbles and falls, and still make him the *"the stone upon which I will build my church."*

Peter, son of Jonas, was a fisherman when he encountered Jesus on the shores of the Sea of Galilee along with his brother named Andrew and business partner James the son of Zebedee. As a disciple of Jesus Christ, Peter was prominent in the early church and was the de facto leader among all of other apostles. He

122

was originally born Simeon, which means "hearing , reed like or grass like hinting perhaps at his human weakness and how easily he was swayed by wind of the world. Jesus later addressed him as 'Peter', "a rock" or "stone." The gospels indicate that Peter initially lived by Bethsaida and later moved to a house at Capernaum which belonged to himself or to his mother-in-law. It couldn't have been a small house because at some point he hosted Jesus and His disciples along with multitudes who were attracted by the multiple healing works. One can imagine that he must have been a comfortable businessman. We do know he was one of the first to follow Jesus. Strangely, immediately Jesus saw him there was a holy connection and Jesus added Cephas to his name.

> *"Again the next day after John stood, and two of his disciples; And looking upon Jesus as he walked, he saith, Behold the Lamb of God! And the two disciples heard him speak, and they followed Jesus. Then Jesus turned, and saw them following, and saith unto them, What seek ye? They said*

123

unto him, Rabbi, (which is to say, being interpreted, Master,) where dwellest thou? He saith unto them, Come and see. They came and saw where he dwelt, and abode with him that day: for it was about the tenth hour. One of the two which heard John speak, and followed him, was Andrew, Simon Peter's brother. He first findeth his own brother Simon, and saith unto him, We have found the Messias, which is, being interpreted, the Christ. And he brought him to Jesus. And when Jesus beheld him, he said, Thou art Simon the son of Jona: thou shalt be called Cephas, which is by interpretation, a stone."
- **John 1:35-42**

Everything about him shows Peter was a leader among the disciples. His love for Jesus and the truth was contagious. He saw the Lord walk on water - and joined Him; he healed the sick and performed miracles also when he

124

went out on a field trip with the seventy; he physically stood up to defend Jesus when He was being arrested at Gethsemane; and in his carnal mind wanted to see more manifestations of deliverance from the hands of the enemies when the attack on their ministry began to grow.

It would seem he did not know that destinies are constantly under fire, although it is the person who stands the test of time doing God's will who prevails even when it seems in the sight of men that they are losing the battle. He had to learn this firsthand from Jesus when Jesus rebuked him for trying to interfere with God's divine purpose in His life.

One with God is a majority.
At the point when Peter wondered why the master kept talking about his suffering, humiliation, and death , he impulsively rejected the announcements just like any of us will be quick to say "God forbid," or "that's not my portion" when we come across something we don't like or when something someone says sounds negative or unexciting. We do not blame Peter here; human beings

naturally are not predisposed to suffering per se, and they certainly aren't naturally keen on spiritual things.

God doesn't think the same way we do, and we not surprisingly aren't able to process things as human beings the same way God processes them. Statements like "unless a grain of wheat fall to the ground and die" may make sense from an agricultural perspective, but it may become something to struggle with when we consider that Jesus was speaking about Himself in that passage, as well as anyone who is going to live their life for Him:

> *"And Jesus answered them, saying, The hour is come, that the Son of man should be glorified. Verily, verily, I say unto you, Except a corn of wheat fall into the ground and die, it abideth alone: but if it die, it bringeth forth much fruit. He that loveth his life shall lose it; and he that hateth his life in this world shall keep it unto life eternal. If any man serve me, let him follow me; and where I am, there shall*

126

also my servant be: if any man serve me, him will my Father honour." - **John 12:23-26**

It takes the supernatural to bear discomfort willingly for the sake of the kingdom of God. In fact people will think you are not normal. You may find people who should be supporting you in such a situation turning their backs and walking away from you; but that's even easier than when they also turn around to be the very persons persecuting you. It is easier for us to carry the gospel of relaxation than that of sacrificial living like Jesus did. But if we know that destiny is meant to be under fire a lot of the time in order for it to be fully manifest, we will learn to stand and face the challenge… and teach others to do so as well. Our churches will teach these lessons more fervently, preparing our young boys and girls to

"speak with the enemy at the gate," (Psalms 127)

A young missionary, heir to a massive estate, once decided to walk a path not too different from that of Moses when he got the revelation of his purpose in Egypt. Not surprisingly, the young man was recorded to 'have thrown

127

himself away as a missionary'. After graduating from high school his extraordinarily wealthy parents gave him a gift of a trip round the world in fantastic luxury and enjoyment for the 16-year-old. However, while on the trip the young man observed much suffering and began to develop a growing burden for the hurting people of the world around him.

1905, this young man later attended the prestigious Yale University, and even right there his classmates could see a man who was so concentrated spiritually, far ahead of them all because of his deep relationship with Jesus, that most began to look up to him as a man to live an outstanding and influential life for Jesus. He had a motto which was, "Say 'No' to self and 'Yes' to Jesus every time."

Comfort can be a big hindrance to what God has purposed to do in the lives of people. As a matter of fact, today it *is* a big hindrance to many people's service to God, so much so that we need to ask ourselves and others if we can sacrifice our comfort for the sake of our faith. Most cannot do this any longer. Some even refuse to acknowledge that God can require them to abandon the things that they hold dear in the pursuit of something much better, even though it does not look that way.

Is it still possible to say "You take the whole world and give me Jesus?" in this present day? Nowadays Narcissism has taken over the body of Christ. We have Christians running like scared cats at the mention of persecution and loss. We have 'notable' men of God teaching the gospel according to prosperity on the pulpits...

Peter too was quick to say "No, my Master will not die such a humbling death. We will give it whatever it will take." But the question he should have asked was, was this thing the will of God for Jesus at that time? Yes, it was; and I'd bet his actions would have been somewhat different had he had that understanding within him at the time.

The Crude Form of Peter
How dare they arrest the master? He would not take the insult!
In John 18:1-12 our bold and impulsive Peter was daring enough to cut off the right ear of the servant of the high priest, only to be chided gently again by Jesus:

"*Put up thy sword into the sheath: the cup which my Father hath given me, shall I not drink it?*"

For Peter it was destiny under fire; for Jesus it was destiny under fire. The Passion – His arrest, suffering, and crucifixion – was a terrible thing that could have been averted if Jesus decided to, but the love of His Father constrained him to walk the bitter path to the cross so that as many as believe in Him can be saved. Jesus saw the big picture and understood the necessity. At this point He was resolute: having prayed the "not my will but thine be done" prayer, Jesus had set his face "like flint" (Isaiah 50:7), determined that nothing was going to shake His resolve.

Peter was a child in things of the spirit, and this was a tough pill to swallow – one that he was not prepared to!

I charge you to try and count how many things you have had to let go of because of Jesus or in lieu of the big picture God has shown you. If they aren't much or painful, you may still have a good distance to go before your destiny is cooked enough under fire and you get a reprieve. Like Peter are you boasting and bragging, saying you are never going to let something happen which God may have intended for your life? It is no *longer about you but about Him who has called you out of* darkness into His marvelous light, and you need to understand this at a very elemental level if you want to have any hope of attaining your purpose on earth.

Chapter 8

PETER UNDER FIRE:

Like Wheat He was Taken Apart

God uses fire (the oven experience) to purify our character and attitude towards Him so that we can be like Him. Peter was such a Sanguine, highly emotional fellow who talked from his head and was very active. This made him rather susceptible to impulses from the flesh, and it was not easy for him to succeed in his walk with God because his love for God was constantly being tried.

1. When Jesus predicted that there was a traitor amongst them Peter was ready to deal with him, quietly urging the master to call out the name of the person.

2. When the Master gave the warning and told Peter that he was going to deny him three times before dawn, Peter did not soft pedal to think twice rather he

went on to brag that it could not happen.

3. When Jesus was transfigured at Mount Olives, Peter was the first to declare that they should remain there and build tents – monuments – unto Jesus, Moses, and Elijah.

This was Peter – impulsive and presumptuous; passionate about his Master, but unbridled to the point of vulnerability and compulsiveness, which are sometimes not divinely inspired. Jesus saw the value in him and purposed to build the Church using Peter as a great leader (Matthew 16:18). Satan saw the value in Peter also and purposed to destroy him quickly, so that Jesus had to step in and intercede to preserve Peter's *destiny under fire* (Luke 22:31-32).

> *"And as they were eating, Jesus took bread, and blessed it, and brake it, and gave it to the disciples, and said, Take, eat; this is my body. And he took the cup, and gave thanks, and gave it to them, saying, Drink ye all of it; for this is my*

blood of the new testament, which is shed for many for the remission of sins. But I say unto you, I will not drink henceforth of this fruit of the vine, until that day when I drink it new with you in my Father's kingdom. And when they had sung a hymn, they went out into the Mount of Olives. Then saith Jesus unto them, all ye shall be offended because of me this night: for it is written, I will smite the shepherd, and the sheep of the flock shall be scattered abroad. But after I am risen again, I will go before you into Galilee. Peter answered and said unto him, Though all men shall be offended3 because of thee, yet will I never be offended. Jesus said unto him, Verily I say unto thee, That this night, before the cock crow, thou shalt deny me thrice. Peter said unto him, Though I should die with thee,

*yet will I not deny thee.
Likewise also said all the
disciples."*
-        **Matthew 26:26-35**

It was a timely warning and Peter was
supposed to take a cue from it, but he was too
focused on his indignation. He failed to
understand it because of his impulsiveness
and this was nearly the end of him – *before he
even really started*. Evidently Peter never
thought he would stumble, a common pitfall
in the lives of many impetuous young
ministers in the Lord's vineyard in modern
times. That is why the Bible warns:
**"Wherefore let him that thinketh
he standeth take heed lest he
fall."- 1 Corinthians 10_12**

It cannot be said any more simply. Just when
you think you've got it all covered with the
devil, that is when you need to be more
vigilant. Our entire sufficiency and
dependence is on the Holy Spirit, and without
Him we cannot do anything. Peter thought he
had it all together but he did not, and it took
him embarrassing himself before his eyes
cleared. He wept bitterly, but it turned out this

135

was a critical turning point in his life.

By the time Jesus was taken away, the flock indeed had scattered like Jesus prophesied and only Peter stood around, but then following only from afar. And when a young lad pointed at him as a follower of Jesus, he quickly denied, not once but thrice! Turns out he was not as bold as he thought.

I wonder how many of us will stand up for Jesus in such moments when nobody is watching and our lives are potentially on the line.

Recently in Northern Nigeria, the brethren's faith were tested when folks were ordered to stand up for Jesus *and* be beheaded. I'm both heartened and saddened to report that a lot lined up and stood for Jesus, and they were killed.

Our *faith is not a child's play, you want to have this etched into your mind now and always.*

No, we do not live in fear; we live in love.

136

Nevertheless, we must not be unmindful of the devil's devices and his fervent desire to destroy us. Some Christians become martyrs for the Lord and end up giving up their lives in the process; and some eventually do not get rich. We must stand for what we believe. Christianity is no child's play, but serious business. It is more than a gospel of the good and cozy life. Yes, it is part of God's provision for us to live in abundance – part of what Jesus died to bring to us; but there's more, there's a price to pay.

> *"And Jesus answered and said, Verily I say unto you, There is no man that hath left house, or brethren, or sisters, or father, or mother, or wife, or children, or lands, for my sake, and the gospel's, But he shall receive an hundredfold now in this time, houses, and brethren, and sisters, and mothers, and children, and lands, with persecutions; and in the world to come eternal life. But many that are first shall be last; and the last first."*
> -Mark 10:9-31 (*emphasis mine*)

It's more than a suggestion or supposition. It's more than merely a thought – it's a promise, a certainty. I know a lot of pastors and speakers like to dance around this reality in their day teachings, but whether they say it or not it remains part of the Bible and actually a word that Jesus Himself spoke. The servant isn't greater than his master – they can't hate me and like you. If you are going to be like me, they are going to hate you like they hate me. And if you are going to work or walk with me, you have to be prepared to lose it all, *and you will*, otherwise you cannot follow me. But after you have lost it all, you will get it all back *in this world*, although the persecutions will still come with it… before finally you inherit eternal life.

Please quote me. I'm only quoting Jesus. Yours may not be death on the cross like Jesus had to go through, but it can be a big sacrifice. I have found that God may not demand everything from you, but He tends to ask you to let go of the thing you hold most dear. He's a jealous God, you see, and He does not like the idea of anything in your heart – anything in your life – that competes with your affection for and attention to Him. With Abraham, God

138

demanded the child that he loved more than anything in the world, the one he spent twenty five years waiting for. With Joseph God demanded his dreams and aspirations. With Job, it was his pride and self-righteousness. Do you even know what yours is? How far exactly are you ready to go for your God?

Challenges are bound to arise

Many of us are weak like Peter was. Even though he meant to stay and stand for Jesus, he was weak because he was leaning on the arm of flesh and on his own understanding. When Jesus took them to pray just before He was taken, Peter and the other disciples were so carried away with sleep that they slept off and didn't pray a single word. You know it as well as I do: sometimes our weaknesses overtake us and bring us down quicker than we can say 'Hi'. This is why we must spend good time praying in preparation for the future, for the inevitable fire that is coming. It is not when the problem shows up that prayer starts. We pray and prepare for the future while we have strength today.

It happened to Peter and he was both embarrassed and ashamed; and we know that

139

other men probably would have given up on their journey of faith and gone right back home. But first there was God – Jesus – who never ceases to give second chances. I am certain you know more than a few people who have walked away from friends and family because such people betrayed them at important points in their lives. The betrayal was so painful that consciously or unconsciously they purposed in their hearts that they would never again leave themselves exposed to the possibility of such betrayals, and so they cut ties with this person. Not Jesus. Not God. Despite Abraham lying in his own wisdom to protect his own life at the expense of his wife, God never upbraided him. Despite Judah sleeping with his own daughter-in-law, he was still the ancestor of Jesus. Despite Rahab being a harlot, she was still incorporated into the family of Israel. Despite Moses being a murderer, God still purified and used him. Despite David killing Uriah and taking his wife, that woman was still the mother of the next king... by David. That's God; He *"upbraideth not"* (James 1:5).

Secondly, Peter still had the courage to pick himself up and come back to God just as he was, and God was able to use him.

Some of us lack this basic courage. We beat down on ourselves so hard for the errors in our lives that we leave no room for God to reform us. Paul was complicit in the death of Steven, and he also masterminded the arrest and persecution of several Christians in the early Church. This did not stop God from arresting and using him; why do you imagine you're too far gone for God to use you?

Let me put it this way: you aren't.

Peter's case was a clear-cut matter of *Destiny Under Fire*, as I am certain yours is also. Peter faced the fire at different points in life too; his was a journey of ups and downs, as is the case with many Christians in the world today. We go through the valley of the shadow of death; we walk through the fire; and sometimes we have to swim across oceans. Persecutions stem upon us from all sides… but if we keep our gaze on Jesus, He will see us through.

141

> *"As it is written, For thy sake we are killed all the day long; we are accounted as sheep for the slaughter. Nay, in all these things we are more than conquerors through him that loved us."*
> -   ***Romans 8:36-37***

What is the journey of your life like? Is it one step forward and two steps backward? Do you feel frustrated; like nothing you ever do is enough? Never mind, keep at it; because that road is not as easy as some people may have told you it is. Only those who keep going ever reach the destination, and it is those who reach the destination that get the crown. God is not moved by those that stood back on the way – those who draw back unto perdition

> *"Now the just shall live by faith: but if any man draw back, my soul shall have no pleasure in him."*
> -   **Hebrews 10:38**

Can you imagine how Abraham who was to be the father of nations coped with fulfilling his destiny? He faced several challenges, took Lot with him when God did not ask him to do so, told lies on the road – *twice* – about his wife being the sister so that he wouldn't be killed and she abducted. He faced the temptation of taking some of the loot from the war that he was not supposed to take. He fathered a son that was not supposed to be... how much fire can a man withstand in his life time? And aren't we all still under that fire that he fanned to flame because they could no longer wait for the promised heir back then?

What's your story? You sure have some that you are not able to share but it is not enough to give up on.

It is not easy to follow Jesus. Whoever must follow him must take up his cross.

Crosses are not easy to carry. Crosses are shame, rejection, embarrassment, victimization and sacrifices. When Jesus was carrying His cross, He fell under it several times; it was a painful experience because it was heavy. If He was not focused, or did not realize that destinies are never handed out on platters of gold, He could well have given up.

143

O, how we thank God that he was able to complete that journey. Where would we all have been today? No wonder the Bible says except a corn of wheat should fall down and die, it would abide alone. John 12:23-25.

Our destinies will be fiercely tried, but those who do not give up will be winners. No matter how hot the fire is, its purpose is to beautify you and make your life and others beautiful. As for Peter, it took correction, embarrassment, and denial for him to be finally converted from his ways and be counted a worthy Apostle for Christ, and a winning one.

> *"In this you greatly rejoice, though now for a little while you may have had to suffer various trials, so that the authenticity of your faith — more precious than gold, which perishes even though refined by fire — may result in praise, glory, and honor at the revelation of Jesus Christ. Though you have not seen Him, you love Him; and*

144

though you do not see Him now, you believe in Him and rejoice with an inexpressible and glorious joy,"

-    **1 Peter 1:6-8 (Berean study Bible)**

Chapter 9

PETER'S DESTINY RECOVERING AND HEALING OF BAD MEMORIES

Peter's denial of Jesus was not as easy as it seemed. It was not easy on Jesus and neither was it on Peter. To be forewarned is to be forearmed, yet Peter bungled it; and until the cock crowed the third time, Peter did not realize that he was the centerpiece of a cruel attack upon his faith and conscience by the enemy. In Luke's account of the incident, Jesus turned and looked at peter immediately the cock crowed and right there Peter got the message. He had done it - he had denied his Master three times in the space of a few moments. Jesus's look must have pierced into his consciousness, so that Peter immediately covered his face with his garment and wept like a baby. We didn't see anything more about him until resurrection morning. O, how he must have crumbled, spending the nights searching his soul!

When you go through one bad experience, a single moment can last forever in your memory. How much more when you go through several?

Psychologists say many times the decisions we make are based on memories, powerful impulses and recollections that we must work through, because they can trigger positive and negative emotions - ranging from fear to frustration, to anger, joy, shame, helplessness, despair, or even inspiration to greater heights. What kind of memory would this have triggered in Peter's life? It well could have shut him off from moving up in his relationship with God forever. Judas' situation certainly ended him!

Are you allowing those bad memories to fester in your life? Are you right now a product of that failure, that marital breakdown of your parents, or even yours? Are you still a victim of that failure that occurred in school? Were you ever so disgraced that you have not been able to go beyond the memory of it? A lot of men of God have not been able to grow past

147

the memory of those failures.

_____

> *Jesus did not count it against*
> *Peter; rather He pulled him up*
> *and gave him a second chance*
> *so that he could go out there*
> *and help others. You cannot*
> *allow your lousy experiences*
> *to limit you. Absorb that error*
> *that you have made; own the*
> *pain; and then lay it down at*
> *Jesus' feet.*

_____

He will make a masterpiece out of your mess soon, but you are the one who has to allow Him by surrendering to Him. Remember that Jesus had already prophesied that the devil wanted to sift Peter but that He had prayed for him.

There are lessons for us here:

1.   The devil took permission from God to test Peter. Apparently he was granted that permission – not entirely unlike the situation with Job – the devil is not resting on his oars, he walks to and fro looking for whom to devour. He said as much about himself when God asked him back in the book of Job… (Job 1:7). We cannot rest on

148

our oars either; we must always be sober and vigilant (1 Peter 5:8).

2. Never laugh at any child of God who is having problems. It is not our place to knock him down but to lift him up (Galatians 6:2). We **ARE** our brothers' keeper – God establishes this throughout scripture, particularly following Cain's misguided question. It is not an occasion to revel; it is a time to be sober and help our brethren as best we can. Interestingly, this is one of the major requisites for making heaven – just in case we have forgotten (Matthew 25:31-46).

3. Never develop a defeatist mentality, rise up in your inside and fight. According to Proverbs 24:16a the righteous may fall seven times, but he rises up again... Stumbling and falling is actually part of the game. Through it we learn how desperately we need the Holy Spirit to aid us in this walk: His strength is made perfect in our weakness (2 Corinthians 12:9). Although the battle is the Lords we must play our part, and that requires getting back on our feet after we've been

149

beat down by challenges and whatever else, and trusting God to guide us into our next step.

4. Furnish yourself with the word of God which is the sword of the Spirit. It is neither acceptable nor tenable to leave our weapon behind as soldiers for Christ, especially since we are in a battle here on earth. In a battle, an unarmed soldier is dead on arrival and you don't want to be that guy. Arm yourself to fight this good fight of faith, remembering that *"faith cometh by hearing, and hearing by the word of God"* (Romans 10:17).

5 In your fight, keep it at the back of your mind that Jesus has a very powerful role to play in the fight for destiny. You cannot do it on your own, else you will fail. You must come to Jesus and let Him play His own part. In the case of Peter Jesus interceded for Peter. In the case of Christendom as a whole, He is our Head, our Priest, Mediator, and Intercessor. And because He is "I am that I am," we must understand that He is to us whatever we say that He is – whatever we need Him to

be. And if we turn our backs and walk away from Him, He cannot be there for us when we need Him to because He is a perfect Gentleman who never imposes Himself.

6.   Peter still fell despite the prayer but he did not fail completely; he was able to rise back up. You and I both need to remember that even though Jesus is there making intercession for us, we are still going to see trouble from time to time. We will not fail though, if we quickly pick ourselves back up and keep our gaze on Jesus.

7.   Peter was restored to a greater usefulness for Jesus' goal. And so will you be also.

Peter had a second chance.

For Peter, it was new life entirely after he denied Jesus. He did not give up; he was still one of the first set of people that went to see Jesus when he rose again. He did not bury his head in his laps and hide like many will do today. It is easier to hide than stand up to our challenges you know, it is easier to compromise a little but when we face our creditors, face the bills, and own up to our sins, God backs us up.

David was described as a man after God's heart but he fell so many times it would make your head spin. Bringing the ark to Jerusalem the wrong way, doing a census that God did not instruct, killing a man to take his wife... He made lots of mistakes but he never compromised on going back to God. For the period during which he lived he had a sincere revelation and manifestation of the grace of God in his life and thus enjoyed forgiveness many times.

Obviously Jesus did not count the sin against Peter. Destiny had be fulfilled, and in the process they would be occasional stumbles and falls. Nonetheless, all things work together for good for those who love him and are called according to his purpose, and they did for Peter, as they are sure to do for you as well.

> Jonah 2:1-10 ESV
> **"*Then Jonah prayed to the Lord his God from the belly of the fish, saying, "I called out to the Lord, out of my distress, and he answered me; out of the belly of Sheol I cried, and you***

> *heard my voice. For you cast me into the deep, into the heart of the seas, and the flood surrounded me; all your waves and your billows passed over me. Then I said, 'I am driven away from your sight; yet I shall again look upon your holy temple.' The waters closed in over me to take my life; the deep surrounded me; weeds were wrapped about my head."*
>
> -   Jonah 2:1-10 (ESV).

If there is somebody who perhaps should not have gotten a second chance, one could argue that it is Jonah, a man whose heart was so grave towards the city of Nineveh that he had the guts to contend with God over the matter of forgiving them. A true and faithful God who is slow to anger and gracious in mercy however forgave him and GAVE HIM A SECOND CHANCE! More than that, God took the time to teach him the reason why forgiveness was so vital.

Forgiveness of sins is in Jesus' DNA. He does that for us once we repent genuinely, and He wants us to learn to forgive other people like He does. In fact, there is a law in the kingdom of God that says if you can't forgive, do not expect to be forgiven at all.

He says even if you have to forgive a genuine 'repentee' 70 x 7 times *in a day*, you should go ahead and do so because God has done the precise same thing for you.

Has your spouse done it again? You think it's more than the number of times you rejected God's love and nailed Jesus again and again to the cross with the countless sins you committed. You think it's more than the number of horrible thoughts that you permit to go through your mind day in and out, not to mention the nasty deeds and the evil communications? O, you *must* know better. Let us learn to forgive, tapping into the infinite heavenly grace that it takes to do so and keep going. That grace is available today, just be sincere about it.

154

Peter by the time he went through the fire of life in his walk with God, became so dependable, matured, and efficient in his role as the leader of the early church. It was he who taught us in 2 Peter 3:9:

> *"The Lord is not slow to fulfill his promise as some count slowness, but is patient toward you, not wishing that any should perish, but that all should reach repentance."*
> -   2 Peter 3:9

That was his testimony and message, clearly expressing his understanding that it is never too late for you to turn around and do the right thing because God is patiently waiting and creating ways for you to do so. Your chances are *not* over with God – He has another chance for you, only this time, you need to take it!

Divine Confrontation

Peter's sin of denialwas not the end – it was only a bad a beginning. Shortly after, when Jesus had risen, the Lord expressed His confidence and expectation concerning the life of the reborn Peter and went on to state His purpose for Peter's life.

"This is now the third time that Jesus showed himself to his disciples, after that he was risen from the dead. So when they had dined, Jesus saith to Simon Peter, Simon, son of Jonas, lovest thou me more than these? He saith unto him, Yea, Lord; thou knowest that I love thee. He saith unto him, Feed my lambs. He saith to him again the second time, Simon, son of Jonas, lovest thou me? He saith unto him, Yea, Lord; thou knowest that I love thee. He saith unto him, Feed my sheep. He saith unto him the third time, Simon, son of Jonas, lovest thou me? Peter was grieved because he said unto him the third time, Lovest thou me? And he said unto him, Lord, thou knowest all things; thou knowest that I love thee. Jesus saith unto him, Feed my sheep."

- **John 21:14-17**

This holy confrontation reveals two important aspects of our Lord.

1. There is no cover of sin without repentance. He forgives even before we ask but he is thorough in His probation to make sure we truly appreciate to need to overcome bad or evil memories and again, enjoy true fellowship with our dear Lord.

2. He looks beyond our faults and sees our needs. Peter was still stuck with the bad memory of denial and as long as he kept focusing on that picture, Peter was empowering the adversary to cripple him.

This is one reason God requires genuine repentance from sin and total healing from evil conscience or bad memories. The Lord was graciously giving Peter an important key for victory here also. To go beyond our bad memories, we have to look forward to our assignment with God and for Peter, that assignment was to 'feed my sheep'. We serve a capable Savior and Shepherd.

Fulfilling destinies is no bed of roses, but a path that is always fraught with trials which God allows. Every time we have these challenges and it seems God keeps repeating the same test with us, it is surely for a purpose, a reassurance of your love and allegiance to Him, and an affirmation of His confidence that He is able to handle what He has installed in you.

At the Vacation Bible School, the children often read a pledge stating their allegiance to the Bible, which is the word of God. They may not fully comprehend the meaning of what they say, but they say it with glee and they enjoy it. As they grow older and come of age, the meaning of it will dawn on them and the patterns of it will show forth in their lives. In the case of Peter, he was confronted in the midst of others by the Lord of lords who had risen again from the dead. A supernatural man. He felt taken aback when confronted the third time because he believed he had proven beyond all doubt that he loved God so much. Yet the Lord asked again and again until it got to Peter.

Some scholars opine that Jesus asking Peter the question three times recalled for him his three-time denial of Him. Perhaps. Right here he was already devoted to Jesus but was still full of self – still forward, quick to comment, and impulsive – but the love of Jesus, characterized by humility, obedience and dependence was already at work in him, compelling him to become more of what Jesus had intended. It certainly does not make much sense for you to be unstable and inconsistent in your walk with God. If you are still in that stage in your walk of faith, Jesus cannot depend on you or commit a big assignment to your hands? It does not matter what you are going through, stability in Christ is one of the first things that you must achieve by his grace although a lot depends on you!

Costly Testimony.
In his walk with God, Jesus had even prophesied Peter's death to him at that time.

> *'Truly, truly, I tell you, when you were young, you dressed yourself and walked where you wanted; but when you are old, you will stretch out your hands, and someone else will dress you and lead you where you do not want to go.' Jesus said this to indicate the kind of death by which Peter would glorify God. After He had said this, He told him, "Follow*

159

> *Me." Peter turned and saw the disciple whom Jesus loved following them. He was the one who had leaned back against Jesus at the supper to ask, "'Lord, who is going to betray You?"*
> -   **John 18 to 19**

Why did Jesus make such a costly prophecy? To show that he was one with Christ? Jesus needed to remind him that he would not be around forever; And that there was a serious assignment ahead of him. With this, Jesus gave him a clear prophecy:

He was going to live very long. His death was going to glorify God.

And true to Jesus words it all came to pass. Peter's testimony was a costly one and we still talk about it today. What will be your testimony? How deeply do you want what the master wants and how far do you intend going with Him?   Tough questions that require answers.

Part **3**

GOD'S LOVE MAKES
THE DIFFERENCE!

Chapter 10

RESPONDING TO THE LOVE OF GOD

God is in love with us. It is not a love that started today but it is one that has been since the foundation of the earth. God's motive for our creation is love; He created us to love and fellowship with Him. Even when it did not seem to work out and Adam and Eve committed sin, He brought out the big stick doled out the punishment but did not leave them exposed. It was a bad deal but God in his manifold wisdom did not think twice before he forgave them and made the first blood sacrifice- He killed an animal and covered them with the skin derived from it. This was the first sacrifice and pointed to Calvary.

As if that was not good enough, He made another sacrifice some thousand years down the road. What happened, the earlier sacrifice he made for Adam and Eve was not good enough to cover up for the sin of all men, to cover up for the sins of the seed of Abraham. All men automatically became sinners through the sin of Adam. They became depraved, no longer the saints he created- All have sinned and come short of the glory of God.

It was so bad that God in a bid to help humanity sent his only begotten son to the world so that as many as believe in Him, He gave power to become the Sons of God. His only begotten son died for our sin to be taken away! Alleluia-(Rom 5:8). He did not just die but was beaten and disgraced. As if it was not bad enough- He was hung on the cross of Calvary!

The ultimate price was paid for the sins of human kind. How else will God show love? How much do you love your neighbor where you live? How much do you love that church member of yours that you serve in the same department and you have lots of things in common with? Are you able to donate your kidney for him? Will you allow your one and only son to donate his kidney to his friend in

163

school? Some people cannot even donate blood, but God came down in form of man, in the name of Jesus as a son to take all the beating from men that he created. It is like the porter dying for the clay when he can discard it and get another clay. This is an aberration but it happened. The blood of God's Son was shed for us. That blood alone took care of so much in our lives!

God still shows us today that He loves us and He cares for us. He still goes all the way. The Bible teaches that God is love. What does this mean? There is no greater love than a man laying down his life for his friends. Do we have the capacity to love Him like He loves us?

What Does Loving Him Mean?
Loving Him means first accepting and receiving His love and the liberty that comes with His love. It means responding to His love. Our duty is simply to respond to the love that God showed to us first. It is just like a husband that really loves his wife with all his life and the wife is the type that brings up irrelevant issues and want an out every now and then because she is never sure of the

husband's love. No, the husband loves but she has not accepted the love and therefore cannot bask in that love at all. Take Note.

To Love God is to put Him First. The book of Mark 12:30 *says* '***Love the Lord your God with all your heart and with all your soul and with all your mind and with all your strength!*** This is a reflection of the commandment of God's in Deuteronomy 6:5. ***You shall love the Lord your God with all your heart and mind and with all your soul and with all your strength [your entire being]. These words, which I am commanding you today, shall be [written] on your heart and mind***

This kind of love is an undivided love that is expected to reflect in every area of our lives.

1. **The love of God must reflect in our desires**. Desire is a sense of longing or hoping for a person, object, or outcome. The same sense is expressed by emotions. Our loving God is not a head knowledge or a piece of idea because loving Him involves our hearts and emotion. I wonder at people who are Christians but who seldom

165

reach out to the things of God in loving Him.

2. **The love of God must show in our affection.** We must cultivate the habit of loving what God loves and must value what He values.

3. **The love of God must show in our purpose.** There is a lot on God's purpose for our lives. It is important that our purpose aligns with his purpose. Make up your mind to pursue those things that he would want you to pursue.

4. **Loving God must reflect in our will.** Our will represent our choice, our decisions. Every man has a will, and no matter what, God never forces his will down on us. We always have choices and abilities to decide what we want and like. Even in faith, the gospel is presented and you have a choice. How much more of when you are now in the faith, the truth is ever presented and you are always left with a choice of whether to do it this way or that. So when we are given a choice to love God in our will, it really is a big test of faith.

5. **We are also to show our love for God in our feelings.** Can you imagine, even at the realm of the emotion the love of God is reflected. Everything counts to God. This is simple- subject your feelings to the truth of God's word. Emotions are there but decisions cannot be based on feelings. We must be in control of our feelings all the time.

6. **The love of God reflects in our character.** We must deliberately pursue holiness, godliness and purity.

7. **The love of God reflects in our thoughts.** We must meditate on the truth of God's word and live every day in the light of it.

Let us take note that love does not stay in the mind, even though it may start from there. Love is seen in our actions- greetings, teachings, writings, playing, working etc.

1 John 4:19 **'we love because He first loved us'** Nobody has a capacity to love God. Our love for God is primarily a response to the

incomparable love that God has shown us in his Son Jesus. We can visualize his dying on the roman cross, but how about the making of himself of no reputation there?

Chapter 11

LOVING GOD IS COMMITMENT

A revelation is a deep insight into a matter, person or subject. It can be anything. Wc need to have a revelation of the fact that we can only respond to his love that has been shed abroad in our hearts by the Holy Spirit. Having this makes it easier to respond to God's love. This revelation also changes everything as we are delivered from performance mentality to a responsive disposition. As we realize this, the true value of His person grows in us as we understand him better through His word and the revelation by the Holy Spirit. This revelation causes us to love Him better and delivers us from our fears and that of the enemy. All these lead us on the true part of love which is commitment to Him and His cause.

Commitment

Commitment refers to a promise or agreement to do something in the future. We can also view this as a state of being pledged or engaged. Other synonyms to this may be allegiance, commitment or dedication. Words like loyalty, devoir, guarantee, obligation also comes to mind. It is staying dedicated to something after the feelings are long gone.

Paul was a committed disciple. Although most of them were committed, Paul's case was special bearing where he was coming from, from the opposite direction. He was one of Gamaliel's disciples and he must have been a high ranking, intelligent one.

Paul lived a life of total commitment since he met the Lord Jesus Christ. He had a special call as we see in the Book of Acts 9:13-16.

> *But Ananias answered, "Lord, I have heard from many people about this man, especially how much suffering and evil he has brought on Your saints (God's people) at Jerusalem; and here [in Damascus] he has*

170

> *authority from the high priests*
> *to put in chains all who call on*
> *Your name [confessing You as*
> *Savior]."But the Lord said to*
> *him, "Go, for this man is a*
> *[deliberately] chosen*
> *instrument of Mine, to bear My*
> *name before the Gentiles and*
> *kings and the sons of Israel;*
> *for I will make clear to him*
> *how much he must suffer and*
> *endure for My name's sake."*

God had made up his mind concerning the purpose for his life. We all have purpose to fulfill and it is very important that we discover our purpose and fulfill it. This instruction was given to Ananias to go preach the message to Saul for a particular reason. Have you found out what your purpose is, if you do not know you cannot be committed? Your call may not be as dramatic as Paul's was, but a call is a call.

Take it seriously. Verse 19:20 says immediately- The encounter makes the difference, he immediately started proclaiming Jesus as the Son of God. He confounded the Jews by proving that Jesus is the messiah.

He showed a total commitment even when the disciples did not accept him, but one thing worth listening to from his story is that God had planted Barnabas the encourager to be a help to him- Barnabas was God's help- destiny helper to him. May we be careful not to miss or ignore our helpers! Our God sent!

2. People stop on their track or they stop witnessing once they speak to someone and no favorable result is realized. How many times have you accepted discouragement to take away the sail from your wind because someone said something? Paul went all the way out. This is a story of commitment to God's love because of the joy of salvation.

It was not all rosy in his life. He was not satisfied with being saved and heaven bound. He encountered every challenge you can think of. He experienced a great deal of suffering.Read what he says in Colossians 1:24

> *"Who now rejoice in my sufferings for you, and fill up*

172

that which is behind of the afflictions of Christ in my flesh for his body's sake, which is the church "(KJV)

Now I rejoice in my sufferings on your behalf. And with my own body I supplement whatever is lacking [on our part] of Christ's afflictions, on behalf of His body, which is the church. (AMP)

2Corinthians 11:22-29 *"Are they Hebrews? so am I. Are they Israelites? so am I. Are they the seed of Abraham? so am I. Are they ministers of Christ? (I speak as a fool) I am more; in labours more abundant, in stripes above measure, in prisons more frequent, in deaths oft. Of the Jews five times received I forty stripes save one. Thrice was I beaten with rods, once was I stoned, thrice I suffered shipwreck, a night and a day I*

173

have been in the deep In journeying often, in perils of waters, in perils of robbers, in perils by mine own countrymen, in perils by the heathen, in perils in the city, in perils in the wilderness, in perils in the sea, in perils among false brethren;In weariness and painfulness, in watching often, in hunger and thirst, in fasting often, in cold and nakedness. Beside those things that are without, that which cometh upon me daily, the care of all the churches. Who is weak, and I am not weak? who is offended, and I burn not?

He was committed to the point of death. A disciple whose hope ends in this life cannot be committed. He will rather be bordered about what people are saying or about pleasing the people around.

There is need to be conscious of pleasing God because we are just strangers on earth. Phil 1:19-20.

'For I know that through your prayers and the help given by the spirit of Jesus Christ, what has happened to me will turn out for my deliverance. I eagerly expect and know that there is no way I will be ashamed, but will have sufficient courage so that now as always Christ will be exalted in my body whether by life or by death''.

How much commitment can we give to God? Paul our example went all the way to the extent that he considered what happens even at death. He believes that even in death, he should please the Lord Phil 2:5-8.

Have this same attitude in yourselves which was in Christ Jesus [look to Him as your example in selfless humility], who, although He existed in the form and unchanging essence of God [as One with Him, possessing the fullness of all the divine attributes—the entire nature of deity], did not regard equality with God a

175

thing to be grasped or asserted [as if He did not already possess it, or was afraid of losing it]; but emptied Himself [without renouncing or diminishing His deity, but only temporarily giving up the outward expression of divine equality and His rightful dignity] by assuming the form of a bond-servant, and being made in the likeness of men [He became completely human but was without sin, being fully God and fully man]. After He was found in [terms of His] outward appearance as a man [for a divinely-appointed time], He humbled Himself [still further] by becoming obedient [to the Father] to the point of death, even death on a cross.

As believers must seek to honor him in death bearing in mind that a believer in Christ does not die but only sleeps.

Chapter 12

DIFFICULT AND TOUGH CHOICES

I wish loving God is such a pleasant and rosy thing. I wish it is just like going shopping in a very big mall with everything in place, several choices, and several people to attend to you. And if you do not enjoy your shopping experience, you step out and move to a preferred mall. What a life of ease and comfort. Or how will faith look like if it is a theater, just acting plays. Unfortunately it was not that straight forward for our Lord even while he was on the surface of the earth and lived like man, how much more of us His followers. That is why we are enjoined to carry our cross and follow him, it is war, it is *Destiny Under Fire.*

Sacrifice- It is a word embedded in our faith. It is woven in every strand of our faith all the way. I wish we don't have to make it, but no, our faith is costly. Loving Jesus is costly, following Him the way He wants us to calls for a life of sacrifice- something young or carnal Christian do not want to hear about. Immature persons in marriage would look forward to having marriage as a bed or roses- a place where you only show love, and have sex as many times as possible- a place of enjoyment. Yes all these are there but my dear friend, marriage calls for abundance of sacrifice from both parties. It is when one person ceaselessly pays the price that problems ensue among couples. Even parent sacrifice a lot for their children in order for them to turn out right, to become what is expected.

In this quest sacrifice means giving to the Lord whatever He requires either of our time, our earthly possessions or even our energies to further His work. Just like willingness to sacrifice is a sign of maturity among the couple, it is an indication of our devotion to God.

Destiny under fire…….. Sacrifice is one of the big sticks that makes the huge fire. It is not usually pleasant. It comes with pain. In Romans 12:1 says

"Therefore I urge you brethren in view of God's mercy to offer your bodies as living scarifies holy and pleasing to God- This is your spiritual act of worship".

In the other chapter Paul made us to know that whether we are alive or we are dead, our own is to honor God. For a Christian, it does not really matter. A sacrifice is not picked from a beautiful shelf and neither does it come in beautiful wrappers. It entails discipline and pain. Just because you are a Christian, you cannot do things the way none Christians do, your standards are higher, and you do not take the place of least resistance. You will need to close your eyes and say No to some pleasure. When it is time to fast, you don't refuse.

When everyone is dressing this way, you may not have that luxury. When scholarship is good in an Islamic Institution, you may have to pay the price of paying fees in another institution while others are having it free. Foul language and evil jesting is forbidden from a child of God but may be convenient for others.

179

Our lives can only change and exemplify the sacrificial lives by renewing our minds. Below I have quoted the writing of Pope Francisco that was delivered at Easter 2017-

A message from the Pope at Mass today. A friend shared it because she found it exciting. I find it so too.
*"You can have defects, be anxious and live irritated sometimes, but **do notforget that your life is the biggest company in the world.** Only **you** can prevent her from going into decline. There are **many who appreciate you, admire you and love you.** I would like you to remember that **to be happy, is not to have a sky without storms, road without accidents, works without fatigue, relationships without disappointments.** To be happy is to find **strength in forgiveness, hope in battles, and security in the box of fear, love in disagreements. Being happy** is not only **valuing the smile, but also reflecting on sadness. It is not just to commemorate success, but to learn lessons in failures.***
It is not just to have joy with applause, but to have joy in anonymity. To be happy is to recognize that life is worth living, despite all the challenges, misunderstandings, and

180

period of crisis. Being happy is not a fatality of destiny, but a conquest for those who know how to travel within their own being. **To be happy** *is to stop being a victim of problems and become an actor in one's own history.* **It is to cross deserts out of itself, but to be able to find an oasis in the recesses of our soul.** *It is to* **thank God every morning** *for the miracle of life.* **Being happy** *is not being afraid of your own feelings.* **It is knowing how talk about yourself.**

It is **courage to hear a "no".**

It is **safe to receive criticism, even if it is unfair.**

It is to **kiss the children, to pamper parents, to have poetic moments with friend, even if they hurt us.**

To be happy is to **let the free, happy and simple creature** *live within each one of us.*

It is to have maturity to say 'I was wrong'.

It is to have the audacity to say 'forgive me'

It is to have sensitivity to express 'I need you'

it is to be able to say 'I love you'

May your life become a garden of opportunity to be happy..... May you be joyous in your spring. In your winter you are friend of wisdom. And when you fall in the way, start all over again. Then you will be more passionate about life. And you will discover that to be happy is not to have a perfect life

But use tear to wear the tolerance.
Use the losses to refine the patience.
Use flaws to sculpt serenity.
Use pain lapping pleasure.
Use obstacles to open the windows of intelligence.
Never give up…
Never give up on the people you love.
Never give up being happy because life is a must-see
Pope Francisco

I asked myself can we achieve all these on our own. Except by the Spirit of the Lord, this cannot be achieved. It is Christ in you that can do all or help one to achieve all that he wrote, not out of flesh. Unless one is truly given to God's word- reading and meditation so that one's mind is renewed, this piece of advice will be a wish, a mirage- another wishful thinking.
Roman 12:2

> **'And do not be conformed to this world [any longer with its**

superficial values and customs], but be transformed and progressively changed [as you mature spiritually] by the renewing of your mind [focusing on godly values and ethical attitudes], so that you may prove [for yourselves] what the will of God is, that which is good and acceptable and perfect [in His plan and purpose for you]'.

We must learn to depend solely on the grace of God and the power of the Holy Spirit to achieve the destiny God has for us. How do you think the Apostles were able to stand for Jesus and died with the truth?

The Book of Hebrews 11:13 makes us to know that some beloved of God died without obtaining the promise yet God was pleased with them. Even in our days many have died for their faith. Look at the people that followed Jesus directly- they made the ultimate sacrifices based on their commitment and love for Jesus. You might need to pray that God, will put his love again in your heart.

183

Not every one of us is called to be a martyr, but who knows, you may be one. Your sacrifice may just be to give more and you are complaining, it may be to help the destitute to support a minister, what God is asking from you today.

> *These people all died controlled and sustained by their faith, but not having received the tangible fulfilment of God's promises, only having seen it and greeted it from a great distance by faith, and all the while acknowledging and confessing that they were strangers and temporary residents and exiles upon the earth .(Heb 11:13)*

1. Did you know that according to this history, James the brother of John, one of his disciples was killed by the sword order of King Herod? Act 12:1-2

2. What about John- The writer of the Book of Revelations? He did not sit down in comfortable and porch office,

with a cup of tea to put down the Book of Revelations. He wrote in pain. He miraculously survived being put into a cauldron of boiling water, but was exiled to the Island of Patmos

3. Peter was crucified upside down.

4. Matthew was slayed by a sword in Ethiopia.
5. James the son of Alpheus was thrown down from a pinnacle of the temple, and then beaten to death with a blacksmith tool.
6. Phillip was hanged.
7. Bartholomew was skinned alive.
8. Andrew was bound to a cross and preached to his persecuted till he died.
9. Thomas was martyred by being run through with a spear.
10. Jude was short dead with arrows.
11. Matthias was first stoned and then beheaded.
12. Mark died in Alexander in Egypt.

All these loved Jesus beyond any doubt. They gave their

*lives for the gospel. Beloved,
there is a price for everything
in life- nothing comes from
nothing. Even the gospel is not
free like it looks on face value.
Jesus paid the price.
Everything that you desire in
your life costs something.*

A beautiful relationship with your wife is
expensive. Writing this book costs something.
You are free to love a Bentley or a limousine
but you must pay the price to own it?

Whether you receive it through inheritance or
a friend's generosity. Somebody paid the
price. The point is if you love Jesus you will
pay the price, you will not run away at any
little temptation or challenge. You have got to
push through. Make the sacrifice today. Drop
those things, attitude or behaviors that draw
you away from getting intimate with God. Pay
the price for your good marriage, for
wonderful children, for great inheritance, for
a heavenly relationship with God.   The price
is nothing compared to the reward after all.

186

Chapter 13

MEN IN THE FIRE!

The Audacity of Faith and Power of Love.

In the third year of the reign of Jehoiakim king of Judah, Nebuchadnezzar king of Babylon came to Jerusalem and besieged it.[2] And the Lord delivered Jehoiakim king of Judah into his hand, along with some of the articles from the temple of God. These he carried off to the temple of his god in Babylonia and put in the treasure house of his god.

Then the king ordered Ashpenaz, chief of his court officials, to bring into the king's service some of the Israelites from the royal family

*and the nobility— young men
without any physical defect,
handsome, showing aptitude
for every kind of learning, well
informed, quick to understand,
and qualified to serve in the
king's palace. He was to teach
them the language and
literature of the
Babylonians. The king
assigned them a daily amount
of food and wine from the
king's table. They were to be
trained for three years, and
after that they were to enter the
king's service.*

*Among those who were chosen
were some from Judah:
Daniel, Hananiah, Mishael
and Azariah. The chief official
gave them new names: to
Daniel, the name
Belteshazzar; to Hananiah,
Shadrach; to Mishael,
Meshach; and to Azariah,
Abednego.*

But Daniel resolved not to defile himself with the royal food and wine, and he asked the chief official for permission not to defile himself this way. [9] Now God had caused the official to show favor and compassion to Daniel, [10] but the official told Daniel, "I am afraid of my lord the king, who has assigned your food and drink. Why should he see you looking worse than the other young men your age? The king would then have my head because of you."

Daniel then said to the guard whom the chief official had appointed over Daniel, Hananiah, Mishael and Azariah, "Please test your servants for ten days: Give us nothing but vegetables to eat and water to drink. Then compare our appearance with that of the young men who eat the royal food, and treat your servants in accordance with what you see.So he agreed to this and tested them for ten days.

The end of the ten days they looked healthier and better nourished than any of the young men who ate the royal food. So the guard took away their choice food and the wine they were to drink and gave them vegetables instead.

To these four young men God gave knowledge and understanding of all kinds of literature and learning. And Daniel could understand visions and dreams of all kinds. At the end of the time set by the king to bring them into his service, the chief official presented them to Nebuchadnezzar. The king talked with them, and he found none equal to Daniel,

Hananiah, Mishael and Azariah; so they entered the king's service. In every matter of wisdom and understanding about which the king questioned them, he found them ten times better than all the magicians and enchanters in his whole kingdom.

And Daniel remained there until the first year of King Cyrus.

This is about the story of Meshach, Shedrach and Abednego, the three Hebrew children that were captured as slaves and taken to Babylon as byproduct of King Nebuchadnezzar's victory over Judah. They were menof rare faith and they brought so much honor and glory to the God of Israel, our God. They were slaves in Nebuchadnezzar's court but they rose to become leaders in that society. Daniel became a prime minister. They all served as government officials in this foreign land where they were exiled.

The news of God's several deliverances and

the exploits of the children of Israel travelled far and near consequently generating all sorts of emotions on the hearers. Some became very fearful and would not want to have anything to do with the Israelites; some wanted a piece of the action and wanted favors from them. To some of the people like Daniel and his team members it generated faith, the type that withstood in resistance Nebuchadnezzar's ungodly demand. They must have heard so much about how their God led them out of Egypt using Moses, heard about Samson, Barak and many others.

What have you heard about God? How much are you willing to stick your neck out in faith? What comes to mind when the office politics begins to get so hot and you feel like quitting, what happens when your child is so sick and you are asking where God is? In the case when you suddenly begin to get frustrated over your marriage and you are almost tempted to run out of town abandoning the whole thing, what do you do at such instance? Daniel and the other three Hebrew men's challenges were not any better or any worse than any of these. It was a test of faith, a test of believe, a test of value. He could have died and everyone forgotten about him if he God did not intervene or he could have compromised and disappointed heaven. We all have choices, in fact we are faced with choices every day. I want you to know that no matter what you face, it is still better to stick with God that you know because Jeremiah 29:11 teaches that **"His thoughts for us are that of good and not evil to give us a future and a hope."**

I love psalm 91, the words are powerful, and outstanding words just like every other aspect of the Bible when we have a revelation on what they actually mean. There has been so much debate on who the writer is, but obviously many scholars concluded that it was written by Moses. Moses? What did he not experience, what kind of fire experience did he not pass through? His destiny was under fire perpetually.

Was it the journey through the wilderness with snakes and scorpions and many more in the wild? Did you ever stop to think of the climatic hazards, diseases or was it political enemies? God delivered them from all;

193

no wonder the beautiful, profound ornamented psalm 91 was put to paper.

He who dwells in the shelter of the Most High Will remain secure and rest in the shadow of the Almighty [whose power no enemy can withstand].

I will say of the Lord, "He is my refuge and my fortress, My God, in whom I trust [with great confidence, and on whom I rely]!"

For He will save you from the trap of the fowler, And from the deadly pestilence.

He will cover you and completely protect you with His pinions, And under His wings you will find refuge; His faithfulness is a shield and a wall.

You will not be afraid of the terror of night,

194

Nor of the arrow that flies by day,

Nor of the pestilence that stalks in darkness,
Nor of the destruction (sudden death) that lays waste at noons.

A thousand may fall at your side And ten thousand at your right hand,
But danger will not come near you.

You will only [be a spectator as you] look on with your eyes and witness the [divine] repayment of the wicked [as you watch safely from the shelter of the Most High].

Because you have made the Lord, [who is] my refuge, even the Most High, your dwelling place,

No evil will befall you, Nor will any plague come near your tent.

For He will command His angels in regard to you, To protect and defend and guard you in all your ways [of obedience and service].

They will lift you up in their hands, So that you do not [even] strike your foot against a stone.

You will tread upon the lion and cobra; The young lion and the serpent you will trample underfoot.

"Because he set his love on Me, therefore I will save him; I will set him [securely] on high, because he knows My name [he confidently trusts and relies on Me, knowing I will never abandon him, no, never].

"He will call upon Me, and I will answer him; I will be with him in trouble;

I will rescue him and honor him.
"With a long life I will satisfy him

And I will let him see My salvation."(AMP)

These young men beyond just faith, they showed their commitment, loyalty, believe in eternity, willingness to sacrifice and believe in total ability of God to deliver when need be.

Sing the Lord's Song Anyway

When the challenge was thrown at the three Hebrew children in exile, their displayed attitude and behavior indicated a revelation of a true love of God. The lesson here is this, no matter where we find ourselves we must endeavor to loosen up and be at our very best. Let us not sing like the Jews sang in Psalm 137:1-6 wondering how they can sing the Lord's song in a strange land. It is easier to join the Joneses. It is easier to look like everyone. One of the lessons of our faith is found in Matthew 7: 13-14

"Enter through the narrow

gate. For wide is the gate and broad and easy to travel is the path that leads the way to destruction and eternal loss, and there are many who enter through it. But small is the gate and narrow and difficult to travel is the path that leads the way to [everlasting] life, and there are few who find it.

It should not surprise you when you find yourself standing alone because of your faith nothing less is expected. God's way. Stand for God even in a strange land. Uphold the standard of God. Do not live a life of compromise thinking that you are not known.

Instead of the compromise these three men stood their ground and refused to bow to this mere metal and stone that they were asked to bow to. Can you stand your ground today in the face of all? They were conversant of the fact that (Ps. 135:15-17) declares that it is wrong to bow to idols even though they knew

198

Nebuchadnezzar was an absolute Monarch-ever powerful King that was feared round the world of them.

The Fasted Life
Fasting is abstaining from food drink and entertainment for a designated period of time in order to create a spiritual benefit. The idea is denial, refrain, forbearance or forgoing for other benefits. In those days children in primary schools were encouraged to fast their refreshments, older ones were encouraged to fast at least a meal a day. The period was expected to create a deeper relationship with God, create a better atmosphere for prayer for during fasting, bodies are submitted to God. In a position of fasting more spiritual power is drawn.

It is a biblical culture that runs from the Old Testament to the new, Even Jesus fasted.
There are different types of fasting.

Standard fast-this is the common fast that we do from morning to evening missing just two meals and breaking with the last meal of the day.
Absolute fast - Jesus went through an

199

absolute fast as he did not eat for forty days.

Partial fast- Here you may eat certain things and avoid certain others.

In the case of Daniel and his friends they chose what they ate and God glorified himself in their lives.

This has thought us so many lessons about diet.

It is not until we fill ourselves with so much carbohydrates that we have eating. They ate vegetables and water and the end result was excellent looks and excellent performance. Today, we have Daniel's fast and Daniels's Diet which is eating only fruits and vegetables for a certain amount of time and abstaining from meat products. Now we do not just use it for spiritual purpose but also as a dieting method.

Daniel then said to the guard whom the chief official had appointed over Daniel, Hananiah, Mishael and Azariah, Please test your servants for ten days: Give us nothing but vegetables to eat and water to drink. [13] Then compare our appearance with that of the young men who eat the royal food, and treat your servants in accordance with what you see." So he agreed to this and tested them for ten days.

At the end of the ten days they looked healthier and better nourished than any of the young men who ate the royal food. So the guard took away their choice food and the wine they were to drink and gave them vegetables instead.
Daniel 1:11-16

Fasting was a usual occurrence in the lives of these young men and that contributed to a major part of their success. They were usually alert and sober. You can imbibe this habit also so that you will be a conqueror.

Enemies

Based on Daniel and his brothers' unfailing love and commitment to God, they were hated by their colleagues. The community could not feign ignorance. The people were conversant of his method and stand about praying to the living God. They were known for success and exceptional testimonies. You will think that should endear them to people, no, it generated enmity among their colleagues. This is a classical work of the flesh.

For many reasons we make enemies. They could be those of our households or from outside. Enemies could be people, policies that are actively opposed or hostile to you. Why do people make enemies? They may hate what you stand for, they may be jealous, they may be instigated by others. Things may have gone sour and swept under the carpet that it could no longer be walked on. It could be ambition, greed, intolerance or prejudice. The devil is the author of them all. Daniel's case was understandable. He had scored so many goals, his success had rendered the magicians in the land as weak and unreliable, his being truthful in his department may have exposed all the secrets and evils that had been covered. Daniel's three friends' positions were firm and uncompromising. It was now the time of their annoyed colleagues to get rid of them. They were very quick to tell the King that the men did not bow down to the image. They were against the new policy.

> ***Destiny was under fire, under trial, challenged to the point of death. It does not matter if your enemies are at work, in the family or in the government. Enemy is enemy, victory is victory. But the Bible teaches that Ps 91:1.***

> ***"He who dwells in the secret place of the most high shall remain stable and fixed under the shadow of the Almighty (whose power no foe can withstand").***

Do not think your foes have unlimited power over you. No they don't it is only a question of time, God will arise and shine in your life.

They were already fed up of their getting good results because God was with them. They won every time they stepped out. The Holy Spirit our counselor is wonderful. You will win again. Key in with your destiny. Enemies? They will always be there, but they are judged already. How I wish they knew.   Proverbs 26:23-27

> *Like a [common] clay vessel covered with the silver dross [making it appear silver when it has no real value]*
>
> *Are burning lips [murmuring manipulative words] and a wicked heart.*
>
> *He who hates, disguises it with his lips,*
> *But he stores up deceit in his heart.*
>
> *When he speaks graciously and kindly [to conceal his malice], do not trust him,*
>
> *For seven abominations are in his heart.*
>
> *Though his hatred covers itself*

with guile and deceit,
His malevolence will be
revealed openly before the
assembly.

Whoever digs a pit [for another
man's feet] will fall into it,
And he who rolls a stone [up a
hill to do mischief], it will come
back on him.

Don't be caught hating people or your
brethren. That takes me to the story of Esther,
Haman and Mordecai, and the attempted
extermination of the Jews. This is found in the
book of Esther. Haman in the position of
power hated the people of God so much that
he hatched a great plan by putting up a terrible
situation to destroy them. Like a series in a
drama, they fasted three days and nights and
prayed led by Esther the queen. God turned
their captivity captive, they had great victory.
Oh what a victory! Haman carried his plot
with his head.

Esther 7:9-10.
Then Harbonah, one of the
eunuchs serving the king said,

"Now look, there are gallows fifty cubits (75 ft.) high standing at Haman's house, which Haman made for Mordecai, whose good warning saved the king." And the king said, "Hang him on it." **So they hanged Haman on the gallows that he had prepared for Mordecai. Then the king's anger subsided.** (Amplified)

In the case of Shedrach, Meshach and Abednego the victory was like another scene in a drama series where the people watching were the King Nebuchadnezzar, his team, the team of reporters that were too glad, to see the end of those young men, ready with their cameras, phones to record the cinema and to send it online and with a great assurance it would go viral before the end of the following day.

It was a bad deal. They did not know who they were dealing with, the God of Israel, the great deliverer. Like the guys knew what would happen, they announced that their God was

206

able to deliver them. I am sure they did not know how their deliverance would come, they threw themselves upon God absolutely. After we have done all, let us trust God. In the face of the terrorists, natural disaster, hunger and all unforeseen enemies. Let us learn to throw ourselves completely upon God.

> ***Enemies may help to put your Destiny under Fire and thereby push you further and further into the hands of grace.***

Joseph's trial was of the devil but manifested as a result of jealousy and envy through the brothers. His father already created the path of jealousy as he made it obvious to the whole family that he had a soft spot for Joseph and Benjamin. Daddy Israel was so passionate he made a coat of many colors for his favorite child. I dare say, Israel opened the door of envy and jealousy in his family. Something that looked good, simple and un-harmful but turned out to be the fire that God would use to bake all of them especially Joseph. He was not only boiled but was baked and grilled in his future experiences. These events were cushioned by the hand of grace as he went through them. They turned to be the provision that God had made to preserve and sustain Israel in the times of famine that wiped out so many.

Are you going through some form of fire experience as a result of your 'enemies'? Not to worry, relax and take a deep breath. 1Corithians 10:13 says

> *No temptation [regardless of its source] has overtaken or enticed you that is not common to human experience [nor is any temptation unusual or beyond human resistance]; but God is faithful [to His word—He is compassionate and trustworthy], and He will not let you be tempted beyond your ability [to resist], but along with the temptation He [has in the past and is now and] will [always] provide the way out as well, so that you will be able to endure it [without yielding, and will overcome temptation with joy].*

You may need to be on the lookout, because the reason for your being under fire right now could be because God is trying to remove some scabies from you so that you will be made whole. That could be found in Galatians 5:19-24.

Now the practices of the sinful nature are clearly evident: they are sexual immorality, impurity, sensuality (total irresponsibility, lack of self-control), idolatry, sorcery, hostility, strife, jealousy, fits of anger, disputes, dissensions, factions [that promote heresies], envy, drunkenness, riotous behavior, and other things like these. I warn you beforehand, just as I did previously, that those who practice such things will not inherit the kingdom of God. But the fruit of the Spirit [the result of His presence within us] is love [unselfish concern for others], joy, [inner] peace, patience [not the ability to wait, but how we act while waiting], kindness, goodness, faithfulness, gentleness, self-control. Against such things there is no law. And those who belong to Christ Jesus have crucified the [l]sinful nature together with its passions and appetites.

209

Watch your responses so that you will also not pay evil for evil. Do not allow un-forgiveness or bitterness to fester, because strife, confusion and many uglies are fruits harvested once you allow strife and anger to prevail see how he puts it in. James 3:14-15,

But if you have bitter jealousy and selfish ambition in your hearts, do not be arrogant, and [as a result] be in defiance of the truth. This [superficial] wisdom is not that which comes down from above, but is earthly (secular), natural (unspiritual), even demonic. For where jealousy and selfish ambition exist, there is disorder [unrest, rebellion] and every evil thing and morally degrading practice

Conclusion.
When, how, why do trials come our ways? Through God, Satan, people, our weakness, our lust, our strength, so many answers.

Have you ever asked the question why me? I am sure Job asked that question when his Destiny was under the heat, maybe like Daniel's companions whose own fire was amplified seven times over in the physical and

210

ended up only consuming the people that went to throw them in the fire.

Job had a very good heart towards the Lord. He devotedly covered all the loose ends on his behalf and on behalf of his family. He was very careful, a perfect organizer who lacked nothing. He was at the top of his game and had it all together. He never expected a raw deal. Even the devil was waiting and was convinced that he was that devoted because of the blessings of God to him. The accuser of the brethren walked up to God and challenged God. He wanted to challenge Job.

After much pressure, in God's infinite mercy and being aware of the kind of Son he had in Job, He gave the devil permission to go ahead, but warned him not to touch his life. This kind of fire was a terrible one, but Job emanated on top. Trials come but God won't leave you alone. In the case of Daniel's trial, it was the King Nebuchadnezzar himself who saw something supernatural in the fire, he saw four men and he asked ' did we not put three men, how come they are four men".(Daniel 3:25)

It is usually said that 'that the greater the trials

211

and challenges, the more remarkable and dramatic, the victories. The end of our trials will remain glorious. Isaiah 54:15 "If anyone fiercely attacks you it will not be from Me. Whoever attacks you will fall because of you. Shedrach, Meshach and Abednego have no smell of smoke, only their ropes were burnt because they are destines under fire. Theirs was more than faith, it went beyond the mere knowledge of the fact that God is able to deliver. They were willing to give up their lives in honor of their God if God so required it. This kind of faith working through love fulfills.

Revelation 12:11
And they have overcome (conquered him by means of the blood of the Lamb and by the utterance of their testimony, for they did not love and cling to life even when faced with death (holding their lives cheap till they had to die for their witnessing. (Amplified Bible)

Our enemies see the God with us even when we do not see Him. Beloved be rest assured that he is always with you in your trials whenever they show up.

Part **4**

DREAM SOME MORE
SOMBODY

Chapter 14

DREAMS

Intangible events and occurrences seen in the mind while sleeping. There are those who believe they are real, and those who contend that they are no more than musings of a tired or overactive mind. For others, it is hard to be certain either way, although there is no denying the fact that dreams do have their impact on daily living for most – if not all – people. (Read about dreams in my book- PROPHETIC GATEWAYS)

Many have seen these night visions and woken up excited or in cold sweats. Some have seen the events that they experience in their dreams come to startling reality mere days or several years after the fact. And for some, they find it easier to make certain decisions based on dreams they have had while they slept!
Of course, they are more than just your imagination. Certain types of dreams may not

proceed from God but they still impact you in ways you may not always be willing to admit. Dreams are 'tell-tale' secrets of the 'hidden places', a glimpse into the NetherRealm – the vast world of spirits. Essentially, dreams show the heart of a situation pertinent to the individual, and when you truly come to think of it, what you are getting is a future or parallel happening regarding something that concerns you.

Yes, even though a lot of people are careless with their dreams, it is important that we all know that what we see in our night visions are arguably even more important than the very happenings in our daily living. You see, the Bible says:

> *"...for the things which are seen are temporal; but the things which are not seen are eternal."*
> -   *2 Corinthians 4:18b*

> *"...that things which are seen were not made of things which do appear."*
> -   *Hebrews 11:3b*

215

One of the ways God speaks to us is through our dreams, which is why sometimes when we wake up from a dream it feels so real. It's because it is real, although not necessarily physical. There are always counterfeits, however, because the devil as usual always attempts to replicate whatever good there is in the work of God and thus corrupt it for his own purpose. There are many who fall into his hands too, because they do not know what to expect or how to deal with the situation. This nevertheless does not alter the fact that dreams are a method by which God speaks to man.

The Bible loads us with examples of people whom God spoke to in their dreams. Joseph son of Jacob was one. Daniel was another. Joseph the father of Jesus. The baker, the butler, the pharaoh, Nebuchadnezzar… it's a pretty long list. For young Joseph, he did not just dream dreams, but he also was imbued with the gift of interpretation and even execution of dreams, so that they quickly became for him a path to victory.

> ***"And Joseph dreamed a dream, and he told it his brethren: and they hated him***

yet the more. And he said unto them, Hear, I pray you, this dream which I have dreamed: For, behold, we were binding sheaves in the field, and, lo, my sheaf arose, and also stood upright; and, behold, your sheaves stood round about, and made obeisance to my sheaf. And his brethren said to him, Shalt thou indeed reign over us? or shalt thou indeed have dominion over us? And they hated him yet the more for his dreams, and for his words. And he dreamed yet another dream, and told it his brethren, and said, Behold, I have dreamed a dream more; and, behold, the sun and the moon and the eleven stars made obeisance to me. And he told it to his father, and to his brethren: and his father rebuked him, and said unto him, What is this dream that thou hast dreamed? Shall I and thy mother and thy

217

> *brethren indeed come to bow*
> *down ourselves to thee to the*
> *earth?"*
> -   *Genesis 37:5-10*

When God intervened in the life of Joseph the husband of Mary, it quickly turned a bad situation into beautiful one, the story of which we still tell today. It had to be devastating for him to learn that she was already found pregnant when he had never laid a finger on her. He could have easily said "tell me another lie Mary," and walked out on her. But a God-visitation to him in a dream changed all that.

Joseph and Mary's relationship carried on through the thick and thin of a humble childbirth, and Egyptian exodus, and the massacre of hundreds of children as he continually stood with her in continuous obedience to the Lord's leading – through dreams!

> *"And having been warned in a*
> *dream not to go back to Herod,*
> *they returned to their country*
> *by another route. When they*
> *had gone, an angel of the Lord*

appeared to Joseph in a dream. 'Get up', he said, 'take the child and his mother and escape to Egypt. Stay there until I tell you, for Herod is going to search for the child to kill him.' So he got up, took the child and his mother during the night and left for Egypt, where he stayed until the death of Herod. And so was fulfilled what the Lord had said through the prophet: 'out of Egypt I called my son'. When Herod realized that he had been outwitted by the Magi, he was furious, and he gave orders to kill all the boys in Bethlehem and its vicinity who were two years old and under, in accordance with time he had learned from the Magi. Then what was said through the prophet Jeremiah was fulfilled: A voice is heard in Ramah weeping and great mourning, Rachel weeping for her children and refusing to be comforted, because they are no more. After Herod died, an angel of the Lord appeared in a dream to Joseph in Egypt and said, 'Get up, take the child and his mother and go to the land of Israel, for those who were trying to take the child's life are dead.' So he got up, took the child and his mother and went to the land of Israel. But when he heard that Archelaus was reigning in Judea in place of his father Herod, he was afraid to go there. Having been warned in a dream, he withdrew to the district of Galilee."

- *Matthew 2:12-22*

O, if only we would all learn to take our dreams more seriously.

Daniel, Solomon and several others were directed in their dreams at one point or the other. In the last days, the Spirit of God would so speak to men that it would not matter whether you are male or female, young or old, married or single; the Spirit will have a free-flow because it is promised of God.

> *"In the last days, God says, I will pour out my spirit on all people. Your sons and daughters will prophesy, your young men will see visions, your old men will dream dreams."*
> -   *Acts 2:17*

Peter was quoting the prophecy in Joel 2:28 as it was coming to pass right there in front of all the people. God keeps His Word – we all ought to know this and believe it with every fiber of our existence. It hardly makes any difference if it is something you read or something you heard; if it came from God, you can take it to the bank.

This is not to say that every dream you have must have a literal interpretation – sometimes the implication is inferred and it will take some digging to decipher. This is not to say either that every dream must have an interpretation from God. We already touched on the fact that the devil is dogged and unrepentant about counterfeiting anything good to further his own purposes. There is also the risk that you could misinterpret your dream and then go get yourself into some kind of trouble. This is why you constantly need to stay in touch with God and surrendered to Him.

If you are the type whom God speaks to in your dreams, you will know when it is God as He will speak to you in a manner that the interpretation will be clear for you, for starters. If this does not happen to be your specific line of gifting, you may want to take your dreams to some elder or more mature person in the Christian faith in order that they might pray for and with you. God could also use them to reveal the meaning of that dream to you.

Following this, He being God, He can then begin to take you on a journey you have never been on before simply because He likes to see people grow in all dimensions. It is not unheard of that God would begin showing you all kinds of dreams that take it a notch higher than what you're used to. When you get this, your response needs to be the same – get deeper on your knees in prayer and submit to Him more. Further, if action is required of you, do it without hesitation or reservation, showcasing that you're deserving of the honor of a closer walk with Him.

Whatever you do, cherish your dreams. They are typically a warning from the unseen world and they should be treated as such because they always have a bearing on this world that we do see. Take every dream seriously and pray about them. Even if the meaning seems obvious, you could well be wrong, so don't act that way. What you want to do is write them down so that you don't forget them, and then pray so that you can act appropriately and adequately when the time comes for you to. Chances are that, because you have yielded to Him right, He will one day take you on a higher ride still... shining more and more, unto the perfect day (Proverbs 4:18).

Chapter 15

JOSEPH, A YOUNG MAN WITH
BIG DREAMS

Rachael and Jacob had been married for a long time without a child between them and they were not happy at all about it, especially since there was this big rivalry in the family over Rachael's sister Leah who was not so loved by Jacob. But Leah was the favored one, who just seemed unable to stop scoring goals in childbirth by giving birth to children every single time her husband touched her.

I have learnt that when such things happen, God always has a special purpose for the persons involved. In this case, the child eventually born to that union was Joseph the dreamer, born to Jacob by Rachael whom he loved dearly and had worked fourteen years to have and to own. How full was their joy despite the ten children already before him! Shortly after, Rachael would capitulate and die in the process of birthing the last child Benjamin, a terrible blow on the patriarch, and by inference entire family. However, Jacob remained consoled by the birth of these two sons and poured all his love on them dearly.

It brought about a significant amount of sibling rivalry, – the kind of love and attention Jacob showered on these two boys. You don't want to do that in your family, dear reader; you don't want to let any of your children feel like they are less loved than the other. It resulted in terrible repercussions for Jacob almost throughout his old age, and that is exactly what happens anywhere we permit that kind of resentment to thrive. The mercies of God did prevail by the time they most needed it, so that all things indeed worked together for the good of the family and that of Israel at large, but this was a complication that perhaps Israel could have done without.

The name Joseph originally means may Jehovah add or give increase and in reality, Jehovah did give the increase which turned things around! Alleluia.

The dream is for an appointed time
Jacob's special love for Joseph and Benjamin incited jealousy in their siblings, and it was not long before hatred followed. This is a word we must not allow to be mentioned in our families because the fruits of it are devastating.

In addition, when your child has a dream, you as the parent must be on the lookout to guide them on what to do with that dream and how to handle it. That dream must be guided; the actions that follow the dream must be guided as well. Don't just listen to the dream and tell the child to go away – stay with them, pray with them, and depending on how old they are, you can interpret it for them and advice on what they should do about it. Joseph's dreams didn't get that kind of guidance or protection; if anything, even his daddy rebuked him at one time.

Frankly, I don't exactly blame Jacob for this – God was taking the entire family through uncharted waters and sometimes wrapping our minds around what God is trying to do can be difficult. Jacob was in the twilight of his years and had had his own walk with God. He

226

had learned his own lessons and was probably just looking to finish out his days in peace and quiet. Then this little boy had to come up with this dream from out of nowhere.

Jacob could remember his own dream a bunch of decades ago, and how the meaning of it had brought him this far. Could it be that Joseph hadn't seen the dream clearly? Or perhaps he had just misunderstood it? Talking about the sun and moon, and stars of sky bowing down to him. Come on, knock it off, Kid!

It could have had something to do with the fact that his mother was no more. There are so many little seemingly insignificant roles mothers play in our lives when we are young and even when we are old. Mothers see things that Daddies miss, and they love their sons enough to give them a second hearing when Daddy is all but done listening to their rhetoric. Parenting is never over, not even when you become an empty-nester. You carry the burden of responsibility all through your life because you're uniquely poised in the life of this person to guide and counsel them as long as you live. What an age then to lose a mother! Many fathers are not as intuitive as mothers,

227

especially in the case of this family with four women to manage. What can one man do among three remaining women all vying for attention for themselves for and twelve grown sons and a daughter? Many times, this man will shoot in the dark trying to manage that family, and many times he will misfire.

Things happen in life that we sometimes are not able to handle, causing us great heart pain. Joseph was purposed to be great according to God's model for his life, so God was going to model him anyway, passing him through an intense fire. Nevertheless, I believe a major reason why Joseph's fire was so extremely hot had something to do with the fact that he was motherless. An intuitive mother would not allow that dream to get into the ear of others at that incubating stage. Like Mary mother of Jesus, she would keep those matters in her heart until the day she is able to say: "whatever He tells you to do, do it."

I know for a fact that a mother's sixth sense would not permit her to accept that her son was dead, torn by some arbitrary beast out in the wild. A mother would have continued searching until she dropped from sheer exhaustion or death.

228

Keep your dreams and nurture them till the time of their manifestation. Whatever you do, don't forget them. Write them down and, as best you can, run with them. They are for an appointed time and they will surely speak. You will then be able to look back on what is written and give all the glory indeed to God.

Now we can't blame young Joseph; he was practically still a child. Daddy didn't get it and Mummy was gone. So, he had all these big brothers that were supposed to have his back but who hated his guts. The young man was groping in the dark here. From the God perspective, it was all just more lemons to squeeze into lemonade. God being more about Destiny Under Fire, he would see all these factors in the young man's life as elements that could be put to use in shaping his life. That's what He does – He takes everything that we are and carefully crafts them in the fire of His formation until we turn into everything that He wants us to be. It can be a slow or a fast process, depending on how aware we are of Him, and how submissive.

That was Joseph's story. Sharing his dreams with the wrong people nearly caused his death

229

but God as usual did not allow that to happen because He sent the slave traders to buy him out of their hands. Daddy had bigger plans – He always does; not just for Li'l Joe, but for the whole nation of Israel. Like, duh! He promised Abraham a bunch of hundred years before that his descendants were going to sojourn as slaves in a strange land. He was just fulfilling His Word in spite of... everything.

Yes, life's circumstances create some of the most intense pressures for us, but it's all just our destiny in our own hands, which can easily be our destiny in our Daddy's hands if we are not too self-willed and opinionated. If you are going to be vessels of honor fit for the master's use, we have got fight for that dream while at the same time yield to the molding of our Father in Heaven.

> *"For the Lord GOD will help me; therefore shall I not be confounded: therefore have I set my face like a flint, and I know that I shall not be ashamed."*
> - **Isaiah 50:7**

230

We've got to learn to trust Him with our dreams because they will create the path for us to follow. Joseph's path was rough. This seventeen-year-old sold into slavery without prior warning was in the fiery furnace of God's forging fires. He could have been killed but God's hands were moving him about within and out of that vicinity, into a place where he or others would have thought that his life was wasting away. But ultimately it was God working him in the fire into a vessel unto honor.

O yes, it was punishment for Joe to leave his prior relationships, his loving father and kid brother, Benjamin; it was punishment to be taken away from everything familiar and comfortable and be taken into that strange land far away where no one know him or cared what happened to him. It was punishment to watch his grandeur dreams fade away into apparent oblivion, wondering how that could ever have happened when this was his reality.

Where are you today? Is everything under control or spiraling out of it? The moving away from that integrated family was actually God's way of protecting Joseph's life and this could very well be the story for you. As a matter of fact, I guarantee that it is. Where you are, is where you need to be at this stage in your life to get to where God has purposed for you to be, because the Bibles says and I quote,"and we know thatall things work together for good for those who love God and are called according to His Purpose". Romans 8:28. However,this is only true for them that love God!

If you love God and have surrendered to Him, then He is the one moving you around. Yes, there were mistakes that you made which you believe you must be suffering for by now. Yes, there are people trying to get atyou throwing their best shots at you all the time. Yes, there is an accuser of the brethren who comes before God to obtain permission to hit you with some bombs, and more often than not, he gets that permission too. But make no mistake about it, not one hair on your head can fall to the ground without His knowing it; and He is watching over your life – over His Word in your life – to perform it… to bring forth your righteousness as the light, and your judgment as the noonday.

See, Joseph's life needed to be protected from the jealousy and wickedness of his siblings while God was crafting him for the place of authority he would eventually be in. Those who were meant to protect him were out to get him, and there could be no room for those distractions while God was shaping this young man's life. They would have conspired again and again to kill him as their malice mounted if he had survived that initial encounter in the well, and somebody perhaps could have hurt him.

The well encounter.
It was a traumatic experience for him no doubt to be cast into some abandoned well by his brothers. Corrupt office politics can get people blackmailed and locked up sometimes when they refuse to play ball with colleagues around them, or when others (wicked folks) are just inspired to snuff you out because they simply cannot stand your jovial and positive demeanor. Those are the kinds of things that can result because of the jealousy of people around you, especially if you are outperforming them and scoring more goals on all fronts. It happens everywhere even on the football field! They could hit you so hard

sometimes that you feel down and low in your spirit, close as you can to being depressed.

It is that time that you need to look unto Jesus the author and finisher of our faith, because you know that He is advocating for you before Father. Because you know that Father also is watching carefully over you to perform His Word in your life and glorify His Name despite the frailties of your flesh. Because you know that Holy Spirit is at work within you to perfect that which has begun. You are sooo not alone – you are surrounded by so great a cloud of witnesses who have gone before, cheering you on and urging you to hold fast to your faith.

Yes sir, your steps are ordered by the Lord, even to the Lion's den. Remember that God has not said there will be no temptationsthat He won't help you to overcome. When you pass through the fires, the Bible promises, it shall not burn you (Isaiah 43:2). Joseph dreamt again and again, and paid a dire price for those dreams every step of the way. And in the end, the vision spoke as, one day, a king called him and asked a question that the flames of affliction had prepared him to answer.

In difficult times, in challenging economies, or when you are going through the supposed hottest part of the oven, just know that it could have been worse, much worse, than all this! Rather than get broken down about it, assume the position of a grateful child and be grateful for life. Be grateful that God has purposed to bless you so much that He allowed for you to go through such affliction. Give Him praise then, instead. Worship Him in your prison chains and stocks. And then watch if God will not tear down the uttermost parts of the earth to bring you unprecedented favor.

Chapter 16

PRAISES OVERPOWER THE HEAT

It was the hottest situation for Paul and Silas that night. The gift of healing with which they worked, and the passion they had for serving God, witnessing, and demonstrating the power of the Holy Ghost was what literally got them into trouble. They could not help the overflow of God's power and anointing in their lives, so that when the Spirit moved within them, they responded, like any good child of the Most High God would. They could not hide or deny it, nor could they cover God's grace upon their ministry. But it came with consequences.

Your light has got to shine and whether people like it or not, folks. It just shines more and more unto the perfect day, and the darkness remains unable to comprehend it. The darkness is going to hate it though, and they are going to try to snuff it out. That shining light shakes up places and gets some people uncomfortable. Folks get healed; complications deleted, problems solved, and works of the devil destroyed. When you are that agent of heaven in a situation, darkness wants to destroy you, so they come at you with some of the worst shots in their arsenal.

Looking back at Joseph, he only had his dreams which he shared with his big brothers; he did not directly offend them. But they were offended by the favoritism showed him by their daddy, plus his dream generated the heat of hatred from family turned enemy. The darkness within them is what struck back in the attempt to snuff him out.

Paul and Silas' good deed of casting out the devil in the young lady remarkably turned into imprisonment for them. The people had them locked in the deepest of the dungeons, bound with the heaviest of the fetters, and prepared for an emergency tribunal on the morning following. Their gift soured the mouths of their enemies and the devil needed to quench their fire in a hurry!

I like it the way the Bible spelt it out: while in

237

the prison, they praised the Lord so much that the chains were broken and the prison doors opened such that they could have escaped if they had wanted to:

> *"Once when we were going to the place of prayer, we were met by a female slave who had a spirit by which she predicted the future. She earned a great deal of money for her owners by fortune-telling. She followed Paul and the rest of us, shouting, 'These men are servants of the Most High God, who are telling you the way to be saved. She kept this up for many days. Finally Paul became so annoyed that he turned round and said to the spirit, In the name of Jesus Christ I command you to come out of her! At that moment the spirit left her. When her owners realized that their hope of making money was gone, they seized Paul and Silas and dragged them into the market-*

place to face the authorities. They brought them before the magistrates and said, These men are Jews, and throwing our city into an uproar by advocating customs unlawful for us Romans to accept or practice. The crowd joined in the attack against Paul and Silas, and the magistrate ordered them to be stripped and beaten with rods. After they had been severely flogged, they were thrown into prison, and the jailer was commanded to guard them carefully. When he received these orders, he put them in the inner cell and fastened their feet in the stocks. About midnight Paul and Silas were praying and singing hymns to God, and the other prisoners were listening to them. Suddenly there was such a violent earthquake that the foundations of the prison were shaken. At once all the prison doors flew open, and

239

everyone's chains came loose.
The jailer woke up, and when
he saw the prison doors open,
he drew his sword and was
about to kill himself because
he thought the prisoners has
escaped. But Paul shouted,
'Don't harm yourself! we are
all here! The jailer called for
light, rushed in and fell
trembling before Paul and
Silas. He then brought them
out and asked, 'Sirs, what must
I do to be saved?"
-        *Acts 16:16-25*

There are a lot of modern-day Christians who
would have done things very differently if
found in this same situation. Many would
have tried very hard not to complain, to keep
their composure and hold the tears back. And
then finally they would have come out with
something like:

"Father, you know that it was because of You
that I got into this mess. You're the one who
said I should go and preach ! And you're the
one who gave me the power to cast out

240

demons. Why are you then allowing all of this to happen to me? Why can't you arise and fight for me, and show all these people that You are the God that I am serving?"

Such words and thoughts are by no means alien to a lot of people out there who find themselves in all kinds of situations today, who wonder how or why God allowed them to get into such messes. We are quick to say things like:

"Father, You know you're the One who told me not to fight. How can this small girl be saying this to me?"

"Father, You know you're the One who said I should take this job. Why am I then getting a query because I didn't want to lie?"

"Father, you asked me to submit to my husband in all things. Does that include when he's cheating, or when he is not responsible?"
"Father, You told me to love my wife. What if she is disrespectful? I can't take this!

But, really? You can't? Could that be why the situation has not gone away? Perhaps God

241

requires you to pass through the valley of the shadow of death in order for you to learn to fear no evil. Perhaps He wants you to be sold as a slave and then locked in prison for thirteen years in preparation for something bigger than you or the tribe that you represent, which He has been working out in your life for ages.

I know this much that rather than complain, Paul and Silas prayed and sang praises to God such that THE PRISONERS HEARD THEM. And as a result, when God showed up, He did not show up quietly – He showed up with a rumble that shook the prison to its foundations. When the situation resolved itself, the same people who had locked them up came and apologized to them. Most importantly an entire family was saved in the process!

Are you in such a terrible situation with your destiny under fire, a situation which you feel you got into because you are trying to obey God and please Him with your life? More importantly, are you complaining about that situation because you feel it should never have happened if God were truly on your side?

Beloved God on your side has never implied that you'll not have issues to deal with. Just ask Israel in the wilderness with a pillar of fire before them at night, yet Balak summoned the greedy Balaam to come curse them. Just ask David fleeing from Saul's wrath in the wilderness despite having been anointed with oil since he was 17 years old. Just ask Jesus' disciples in a storm on Galilee's sea while Christ slept at the bottom of the boat.

When you pass through the waters... or through the fire...!
Perhaps it is time to change tactics and do the opposite. Perhaps it's that time when you give God a praise that bothers the people around you, notwithstanding what you're going through. Perhaps it's time like Job to rend your clothes and declare: "though he slay me, yet will I trust him...!" (Job 13:15).

I guarantee you, when God shows up, He will not show up quietly. It will be with an earthquake that shakes your every prison to its foundation. It will be with a miracle that transforms your enemies into your helpers. And, of course, to the glory of His Name, it will be with a transformation that saves lives –

243

because that is our Daddy's primary business: life everlasting for all.

When you think it is hottest, what it demands is a lot of praise, trust, andfaith. It is that time you must come to acknowledge that your enemies today may have been permitted by God to be your destiny helpers and get you to the next stage. This is a tough nut to crack for too many Christians, but it is only too true. God let's these things happen for our own good, so that we become the best versions of ourselves that we could ever have.

So, when you have done all the things that you know how to do, go an extra mile and begin to praise and worship Him with very fiber of your being! Give Him a praise, a real one. Let the other prisoners hear it. Let the world wonder if you are insane or if there is something wrong with you. And then let's see if Daddy will not shake your situation to its roots because you dared to trust in Him.

Chapter 17

YOUR DREAM PUSHES YOU OUT
OF THE COMFORT ZONE

People are usually pushed to their destinies through suffering. A lot move out of their countries in a bid for greener pasture, some are forced to completely move because nothing was working anymore where they were. And then it turned out that in moving out of suffering and discomfort, they later realized that the unwanted conditions they dealt with was the helper which propelled them into fulfilling their divine purpose in God. The Psalmist declares and I quote, "It is good that I have been afflicted so that I might learn your decrees" Psalm119:71

The caravan traders moved Joseph forward and sold him to an officer of the Pharaoh. This journey of heartbreaks wasn't easy by any means, but the choice of whether or not it happened to him was completely taken out of his hands. All he could do then was just respond, play along – deal with each situation as it presented itself.

Hey, keep your heart; don't allow it to be broken. You're going to need it when God turns your captivity around.

A dear woman at age thirty-five lost her sight right in the middle of her game enjoying what was supposed to be her American dream. Blindness was not part of her initial dream to conquer her world and make every bit of it as comfortable and pleasurable as life in God's Country can be. Then another disaster struck as her husband came home one day to announce he was giving up the fight to be her great husband and consequently leaving her to battle her blindness and raise their little boys alone blind and pitiful. She felt devastated, desolate and a wreck wallowing in daily doses of tears and self-pity. God went to work and gloriously saved her soul. She developed and deployed a new career as a blind multi-lingual interpreter with a sterling reputation as the best in her new game. What more? Her husband repented and returned to her a changed man but the devil was not done.

While basking in her new found faith, Career and marriage the devil struck and her teenage son was murdered in a road rage incident. The justice system inflicted further pain on her by allowing the murderer to go scot free on the pretense of self-defense. By now, our star had totally lost faith in God and man. She was ready to battle even God to a standstill as in her thinking, evils are not supposed to befall Believers in Christ. I have a right to my anger and unforgiveness she shot back at God. In her total despair and fallen state, the good Shepherd went to work restoring her one limb at a time. Today, she is a Preacher of the gospel, a bestselling author and a global conference speaker and boy; she is absolutely hilarious and fabulous. Yes, she passed the difficult test too; that of completely forgiving the murderer of her son. The full story of Janet Perez Eckles and her books can be found on her website; janetperezeckles.com. What am I driving at?

The devil does not stop at inflicting one pain but he keeps trying to get his hands on everything that matters to you. Like he did when he kept working at it in the case of Job, he would like to take your animals, your staff members, your spouse and children, as well as your health – everything he can get permission to touch he will touch. And why? Because he needs you to curse God and die; he needs you to lose your soul to him forever.

Satan was frustrated at Job's faithfulness to God. It irked him, and he needed to prove that Job was serving God only because he was so blessed by God. In many instances too, he would have been right. Concerning too many so-called 'children of God' in modern day, the accuser of the brethren would likely have a point because many indeed are serving God only when things are convenient. Folks don't mind going to Church when the bank account is frolicking, when there are nice clothes to show off, a bulky car to drive, and a wife that says, 'I love you' while she kneels to deliver breakfast. But at the first sign of trouble some will find an excuse to skip Church, pay a bribe, or even commit an abortion.

It's a painful truth, but one that we should not turn our backs on. It's like a kick in the gut each time I read the passage where Job gets the news of the death and destruction of everything that he holds dear – all that he has

248

ever worked for his entire life: GONE! One servant after the other brings in their own devastating news, and each passing second his heart breaks just a little deeper. And in that last moment the news that all his children had died on the same day and at the same time – none surviving.

I almost always have tears in my eyes when I read of Job's response and I ask myself: Can I do this?" "Will I?"

> *"Then Job arose, and rent his mantle,14 and shaved his head, and fell down upon the ground, and worshipped, And said, Naked came I out of my mother's womb, and naked shall I return thither: the LORD gave, and the LORD hath taken away; blessed be the name of the LORD."*
> *- Job 1:20-21*

I brought nothing into this world and I am taking nothing away with me when I leave. Everything I have – or had – was given me by God. Why then should I worry so much that

He chose to take them away. Instead, I will worship and bless Him even more, because He deserves it that much more!

Joseph's matter wasn't all that different at all. Yet he hung in there in Potiphar's house and later in prison. He continued to serve with his whole heart as if his life depended on that service, so that inevitably he was made head everywhere that he was. Was his service going to take him back to his people? No, that was not what God was about. He had not gotten an answer to his own problems but he did what needed to be done by serving with all his might, as though he was serving God Himself.

Do the Needful.
That is the key lesson for all and sundry right there. Wherever you find yourself, whatever your circumstances, give it your best always, all the time. God will show up eventually, and it will not only be on time, but it will also be so big that it will blow your mind. So, give it all it takes.

Further to Joseph's story, it turns out, not only did he interpret the dreams of the baker and butler, but he also made a plea in the effort to get free.

> *"And Joseph said unto him, This is the interpretation of it: The three branches are three days: Yet within three days shall Pharaoh lift up thine head, and restore thee unto thy place: and thou shalt deliver Pharaoh's cup into his hand, after the former manner when thou wast his butler. But think on me when it shall be well with thee, and show kindness, I pray thee, unto me, and make mention of me unto Pharaoh, and bring me out of this house: For indeed I was stolen away out of the land of the Hebrews: and here also have I done nothing that they should put me into the dungeon."*
> -   *Genesis 40:12-14*

See, these are the elements that show that our characters in the Bible are not wooden, plastic, or make-believe characters. They are

251

real human beings with real issues, faced with extraordinary complications that they needed to pull out of one way or another. Making a plea, putting in a word for yourself, is nothing sinful, but it showed that this young man was hurting, and he wasn't impervious to the discomfort. He wanted out, every bit as much as you want out of any suffering you may find yourself having to endure.

I see it as humility and trust in God. Making a request does not mean that you do not trust God and neither does it make you any less holy. It makes you human, and as a matter of fact, it shows that you're surrendered to God's sovereign authority in your life. You're real, you're sincere, and you just need help. In this case, Joseph's thoughts about freedom were much less than God's unfolding plans for him so God blocked the request. Make a request if you need it, particularly if you feel led by the Holy Spirit. Remember as many as are led by the Spirit are the sons of God. Had God allowed Joseph to be free and deported back home to Canaan, it would have been a terrible disruption of nearly twenty years of divine preparation and positioning for greatness. Get all the help you can but let God have His way.

It took three days of fasting and prayers for Esther to gain enough confidence to approach the throne of her husband-king Ahasuerus. But it was what she needed to do, and she did it. She got the results too.

It is going to take something to push you out of the valley, but when it does, don't just sit down there sulking and doing nothing. Get proactive in prayers, and then don't stop doing something until something happens. If you need to appear at a higher court, please do that too. Don't just give in, roll over, and play dead. Timidity is not a virtue in God's kingdom! God is covering His end, but He wants you to cover yours too. Everything you need is already available, but it's not just going to pour out into your hands simply because you want it. It takes pressure to beat pressure, be it spiritually, physically, or otherwise. You want to play your part and do it right.

Ability and intelligence became Joseph's trademarks. He very quickly understood his strengths and played to them. This is important for you too – that you know perfectly what your gifts are and that you put them to good use.

Ask yourself, what are you capable of doing excellently and perhaps independently? Joseph had this thing with dreams, and he used it to help people. He also had a thing for organizing the establishments and running a tight ship. So, he did this first at Potiphar's home and later at the prison. No, he did not rejoice at the predicaments of the butler and the baker. He heard their plights and empathized with them; it was how he came around to interpret their dreams for them.

If you've never gotten this anywhere, get it now – you must never stop at being compassionate and caring for others. Don't rejoice at others' failure. As a matter of fact, it is important for you to understand that all you have been given is for the purpose of being a blessing to others. If you fail to dish out your blessings for the benefit of humanity as a whole, or at least your immediate society, your gift will stagnate and become a corruption even to you (James 5:1-6)

Some folks get so frustrated in trials they buck and stop giving their best. They feel they have worked hard enough and the world around them is too cruel to matter anymore. As their

254

attitudes become nasty, they give room to depression and just stop caring, or acting out their compassion. Naturally, those negatives send people away from them such that these people truly begin to die slowly. The Bible warns about this in Hebrews 12:14-15 when it says, "Follow peace with all men, and holiness, without which no man shall see the Lord: looking diligently looking diligently lest any man fail of the grace of God; lest any ROOT OF BITTERNESS springing up trouble you, and thereby many be defiled…"

A cheerful heart is like good medicine – it can heal you by its own self. But when you allow sorrow and bitterness to take root, they kill. Literally. Folks get ulcers, headaches and migraines, high blood pressure, and all other kinds of diseases. Depression, bipolar disorder, split personality… all these are works of the devil, but even some actual Christians suffer from them when they fail to deal with frustrations that are welling up within them due to complications that they run to in their daily lives.

Yea when the heat is on, you want to stop everything you are doing and fight the battle yourself... as if you were ever built to do that! For the love of God, we wrestle not against flesh and blood, but against principalities, powers, rulers of darkness, and spiritual wickedness in all kinds of places. This is why we have been given weapons that are not canal, but made mighty by our relationship with Christ. We wield these weapons then by focusing on the things that Christ, by the Holy Spirit, instructs us to – positive thoughts, our confession, our relationship and standing with God... all activated through faith.

See, if you get into the habit of allowing the frustrations of life to get through to you, you defeat your own self and everything that God has purposed for you is unable to get to you. Remember, "with joy" is how we're supposed to draw from the wells of salvation. But if your joy is lost, then bitterness gets into your spirit, and such a spirit will make you vengeful. Rather than doing it God's way, you find that you want to retaliate, which puts you firmly in the realm of Satan's machinations.

Never stop using your gifts. Keep them on fire. God is the only one who promotes and rewards, and He intends to do that for you. He will not allow you to be tempted more than you can bear, meaning, if He has let you go through this complication at hand, it is because He trusts that what He has invested in you is good enough to handle the problem at hand. It is actually cause to rejoice. Keep the shine on friend.

"Wisdom is the principal thing; therefore get wisdom: and with all thy getting get understanding. Exalt her, and she shall promote thee: she shall bring thee to honor, when thou dost embrace her. She shall give to thine head an ornament of grace: a crown of glory shall she deliver to thee. Hear, O my son, and receive my sayings; and the years of thy life shall be many. I have taught thee in the way of wisdom; I have led thee in right paths."
- *Proverbs 4:7-11*

"For promotion cometh neither from the east, nor from

> *the west, nor from the south.*
> *But God is the judge: he puts*
> *down one, and sets up*
> *another."*
> -   ***Psalms 75:6-7***

It's just sad to imagine the number of people out there who do not get this little understanding. Some of them even quote these scriptures, but it is evident that they don't have a clue what it means. It is why some folks will get carried away by their accolades and achievements in this world, and it is why some would get so terribly frustrated over certain failures. If we would all but surrender to the sovereignty of God and accept that despite all our hard work it was grace that got us here, we would enjoy life better; and like Job when he got all that terrible news on the same day, we would be able to say, "the Lord giveth and the Lord taketh away; blessed be the Name of the Lord!"

Chapter 18

DEVELOP THE RIGHT ATTITUDE

That's the right attitude right there – I am for Jesus; I belong to Him. My life is not my own; I was created exclusively for His pleasure. He knows who I am and what is best for me; and His purposes for me are better even than my own purposes for myself. Therefore, come rain or shine, plenty or poverty, He is working out constantly what is best for me and I can put my entire trust in Him while worshipping Him with all my heart!

Pursuing your dream will take you out of your comfort zone – you must know that already. You can however never achieve much if you have a bad attitude. Murmuring and complaining, being bitter, angry, and vengeful, hurting others... these are all symptoms of a bad attitude, every bit in the same space as whining. Frankly it is irritating to God, even though it doesn't stop Him from loving you.

These are all characteristics of one primary flaw in most people: selfishness; and they expertly get you nowhere in a hurry. If anything, they add a negative stint to your life, drive away good people from you, and attract even more negative emotions and situations. Like a mile-long trail of exquisitely arrayed dominos, they cascade from one debilitating sentiment to the next until you are completely overwhelmed with frustration. The worst part is that all of this can be going on while you're wearing a very plastic smile on your face, so much so, even you may be unaware that it is eating away at you.

The effects can be devastating. Negative emotions ruin your health and relationships, and it is not very long before they bleed into your life and livelihood. We must consciously avoid this, and the Bible has given us the tools to do so.

> *"Finally, brethren, whatsoever things are true, whatsoever things are honest,1 whatsoever things are just, whatsoever things are*

260

*pure, whatsoever things are
lovely, whatsoever things are
of good report; if there be any
virtue, and if there be any
praise, think on these things. "*
-        *Philippians 4:8*

This is the real warning: it cannot be a passive process. It is active. You must actively focus on the positive things in your life, deliberately put yourself to work on productive things, and consciously silence the negative emotions when they come up. Please get me right – this is not encouraging you to bury your feelings in denial. That is just as devastating as anything else. No, face up to the emotion. As a matter of fact, lock yourself up in your room for a little bit if you feel the need to. Cry your eyes out – it is healthy for you. Then purposefully get back on your feet and put yourself to something productive.

The key is hiding the Word of God in your heart – there is nothing on this planet that is more true, honest, just, pure, lovely, virtuous, of good report, and praise-ful than the Word of God itself. That is the life that breathes inside of you, the life which holds up the world in the middle of nothing; the essence that sustains everything your eyes can see, and the much more that even your mind can't even wrap against. If it can sustain all creation, it can heal you.

Speak that Word to yourself aloud, over and over again to keep your mind in remembrance of it. Look at the specific promises that God has made to you and jump to your feet to dance a jig because suddenly you can feel the excitement creeping back into your veins. "Though my beginning may be small, yet my latter end shall greatly increase." "I will not leave you comfortless; I will come to you…" "The Lord shall fight for you, and you shall hold your peace!" "All things work together for good for them that love God, who are called according to his purpose."

It goes on and on, promise after promise. You begin to realize that you are still here, and even though the heat is turned up on your destiny under fire, you are firmly situated in the hollow of his hands and the fire cannot burn you. Everything you love and hold dear seems to have been taken from you; everything that can go wrong appears to have gone and still be going wrong; you have taken a slap on one cheek, and upon turning the other they have well almost knocked your head off; but still you stand, because Daddy has never once let you go the entire time.

> *"We are troubled on every side, yet not distressed; we are perplexed, but not in despair; Persecuted, but not forsaken; cast down, but not destroyed; Always bearing about in the body the dying of the Lord Jesus, that the life also of Jesus might be made manifest in our body."*
> -   *2 Corinthians 4:8-10*

It's a beautiful thing to know that you're inside of what God is doing and that you're still loved dearly by Him. To know that He has loved you enough to permit you to partake of something as beautiful as His Own sufferings so that you can likewise revel in His unmistakable glory is one of the most mind-boggling feelings a human being can ever have! O, you want to make up your mind that no matter what is going on in your life, you will develop that

263

good attitude which enables you to break out in praise even when the enemy holds a knife to your throat. This will allow God's favor and grace to flow positively into your life and bring about breakthroughs that you could only ever have imagined.

No, Joseph did not keep talking about his past, he moved forward and did his best always, excelling everywhere he went. He lived the present in a very healthy manner while waiting for the future that only God can give.

Chapter 19

AVOID SIN... ZIP IT

The unmanned cookie in the jar.

The devil has that option too – a little sin nobody would notice. Sure, you'll get away with it, you'll be able to eat your cake and have it; to hold on to your vision and still have that sweet memory of a forbidden pleasure on the side – the little secret...

Except, you don't get away with it. Nobody does. God is just too real to let that happen. King David murdered Uriah surreptitiously and looked to get away with having a baby by his captain's wife, but God was having none of that. David was very publicly punished. Abimelech murdered his brothers to become king and ended up being betrayed by his own people before a girl killed him with a millstone. Achan thought he had gotten away with the gold and crimson robe, but the whole of Israel paid dearly for it, just shortly before he was found out and his entire family wiped out.

No, you don't get away with sin, no matter how little, especially if you are on that close personal walk with God. Daddy takes no prisoners when it comes to sin, and He is always harsher about it with those who are closer to Him, just like He said to David when the singing monarch judged himself: "Howbeit, because by this thy deed thou hast given great occasion to the enemies of the Lord to blaspheme..." (2nd Samuel 12:14)

Yes, God put the dreams in our lives. He did the DNA and He is the author of the dream that we have. It is not there in us by mistake. He initiated it by planting the seed and fortifying us with the desire and ability to go get it. Therefore, we must do it his way and not try to take shortcuts. Follow His standard. God created the dream of a Savior in Jesus. It was an excruciating death that was laid upon Him. At a point in Gethsemane, Jesus wished the cup would pass from Him but still prayed, "Not my will but yours be done," (Luke 22:42b). He deferred to doing it God's way; and even though it still hurt – badly – in the end it was worth it for the Church that He birthed and the Crown of Glory that He earned.

266

Too commonly we trivialize the significance of that night in the Garden, when Christ sweated blood and the angel did not show up to strengthen Him until after He had surrendered His (Luke 22:41-44). But that was the moment when Jesus almost broke, literally. By the next hour when the torture started and the passion grew until it was culminated at his giving up of his ghost, it was not as tough as that night when he decided to set his face like flint and despise the shame for you and for me.

That was the moment when Christ overcame the final temptation. But it was by no means the first. The first temptation had been three years earlier, when after forty thirsty days in the wilderness a hungry Jesus was offered all the kingdoms of the world in exchange for the little token of simply bowing down to Satan and worshipping him. He stood firm and did not compromise. Many of us compromise in fulfilling God's dream, you see a businessman pay another man so much bribe to push a competitor out. Ladies come out lustfully or do all manners of evil to get the Job after they have compromised their faith fornicating with their supposed bosses. There was a period that

267

giving bankers targets to bring in some ridiculous amounts of money monthly or faced the risk of losing their jobs was the order of the day in some African countries. Not that it is exactly gone either.

Folks come to Church to pay tithes of monies they stole or cheated others out of. People scream hallelujahs over testimonies of jobs they secured through affairs with the recruitment officer or by qualifications they paid hard cash to obtain. It was bad then, and it still is. Many succeed at the expense of their virginity. Women frolic around, sleeping with men and each other to make enough money for their families. Men engage in lewd acts and even human sacrifices in order to be able to buy the next big 'jeep' on the market...

Too many men think that they have the right to sleep around outside of their marriage... and the media has promoted this all over the world, both local and social. It is just fashionable. But how much has the Bible made it obvious that God hates fornication and adultery? In 1 Corinthians 6:9-20. The word fornication shows up at least 4 times.

"Know ye not that the unrighteous shall not inherit the kingdom of God? Be not deceived: neither fornicators, nor idolaters, nor adulterers, nor effeminate, nor abusers of themselves with mankind, Nor thieves, nor covetous, nor drunkards, nor revilers, nor extortioners, shall inherit the kingdom of God. And such were some of you: but ye are washed, but ye are sanctified, but ye are justified in the name of the Lord Jesus, and by the Spirit of our God.

"All things are lawful unto me, but all things are not expedient: all things are lawful for me, but I will not be brought under the power of any. Meats for the belly, and the belly for meats: but God shall destroy both it and them. Now the body is not for fornication, but for the Lord; and the Lord for the body. And God hath both raised up the Lord, and will also raise up us by his own power. Know ye not that your bodies are the members of Christ? shall I then take the members of Christ, and make them the members of an harlot? God forbid. What? know ye not that he which is joined to an harlot is one body? for two, saith he, shall be one flesh. But he that is joined unto the Lord is one spirit. Flee fornication. Every sin that a

269

man doeth is without the body; but he that committeth fornication sinneth against his own body. What? know ye not that your body is the temple of the Holy Ghost which is in you, which ye have of God, and ye are not your own? For ye are bought with a price: therefore glorify God in your body, and in your spirit, which are God's."

Joseph had a chance to be Mrs. Potiphar's bedmate while her hubby was so busy with issues of state and she had been lonely. I don't know how many young men would have passed that temptation over – the chance, while being a slave, to have a regular person they'd be sleeping with while the boss was away. It would have meant even more promotion by the boss; it would have meant more comforts in the slave quarters; and it would have meant that any time there was a falling out with the master, his wife would come to their defense.

Yes, exactly. It would have meant staying a slave for the rest of their lives– a high-ranking and respected slave, but a slave nonetheless. So many people have sold their birthrights for small comforts along the road to perdition just because they couldn't handle the temptation. "Don't blame me: you don't know what it was like," they would quickly argue. And I would tell them, "You're right. I don't. But God does, and He evidently does not like it." That's why all those warnings about fornication; that's why a passage such as this exists:

> *"There is a way that seemeth right unto a man, but the end thereof are the ways of death."*
> -   *Proverbs 14:12 & 16:25*

Let's learn to do it God's way; we're obligated to. The benefits of holding strong to the end are real, and so are the consequences of copping out and falling by the wayside. A life of compromise with all manners of small sins and big sins will not hasten our dreams to come to pass and would not make us more comfortable. As a matter of fact, it is more likely to destroy us – like it did King Saul when the Lord finally rejected him for thinking more about himself than the instruction he had received from God. We may look comfortable on the outside by succumbing to sin, but we would be dying on the inside, and it is only a question of time

271

before the stench of it breaks out for the entire world to smell.

> *"For this, Thou shalt not commit adultery, Thou shalt not kill, Thou shalt not steal, Thou shalt not bear false witness, Thou shalt not covet; and if there be any other commandment, it is briefly comprehended in this saying, namely, Thou shalt love thy neighbour as thyself. Love worketh no ill to his neighbour: therefore love is the fulfilling of the law."*
> -   *Romans 13:9-10*

Joseph took to his heels and fled from the scene of the proposed crime, a choice for which he paid a dire price – prison.

I can imagine how many modern-day Christians could have come to tell him, "Brother, why didn't you just do it? It would have been just 10 minutes of your time and nobody would have every known about it. You can always go back to God and ask for

272

forgiveness later. Now look what you have done to yourself. Who's going to help you out of prison now?"

If you were watching a movie or even seeing this happen in real life, you would think Joseph was jinxed. It is not uncommon when you're a person of Destiny Under Fire. People will think you are jinxed, and you'll get a lot of those sympathy and solidarity phone calls, folks feeling sorry for you, some pretending to encourage you while secretly gloating, others sincere in their admonition that you stay strong until the God of Shiloh shows up with your recompense.

People may think you are jinxed right now, they may think you are not aggressive enough – it's your laziness, your ignorance, or even plain stupidity on your part. But I assure you that life is a process dear friend, and everybody gets to pass through their own fire. Some, like Shadrach, Meshach, and Abednego, could come out unscathed without even the small of fire on their clothing; while others can cave in and be consumed by the flames because they succumbed to sin. Either way, you cannot hasten the process! It comes

273

with pain, but you need to stay right on it. The pain will inevitably soon be over.

Obedience is costly like that, but the reward is priceless. Joseph endured it and became Prime Minister. David endured and became king. Job endured and was made 10 times better at the end than he was at the beginning. And as for Jesus, He got the name which is above all other names.

Jesus paid that price with His reputation and integrity, a perfect costly obedience. He paid with physical and emotional pains that would cripple most men. But today we are His children forever because He endured that walk to the cross!

Philippians 2:5-11 made it very clear

> *"Let this mind be in you, which was also in Christ Jesus: Who, being in the form of God, thought it not robbery to be equal with God: But made himself of no reputation, and took upon him the form of a servant, and was made in the likeness of men: And being*

274

found in fashion as a man, he humbled himself, and became obedient unto death, even the death of the cross. Wherefore God also hath highly exalted him, and given him a name which is above every name: That at the name of Jesus every knee should bow, of things in heaven, and things in earth, and things under the earth; And that every tongue should confess that Jesus Christ is Lord, to the glory of God the Father."

- *Philippians 2:5-11*

Can you pay that price also? Will you?

You are not paying a price for salvation – that one is free. You are paying the price of mortifying your flesh, the price for a closer walk with God, for a clearer vision and a better understanding of what His will is for you. You are paying the costly price for a cleansing in the furnace of God's fashioning, which transforms you from raw material into decontaminated gold, an able vessel fit to be placed in the Hand of the Master.

If Joseph had compromised, he would never have succeeded in becoming who he eventually did become – more or less a king.

He certainly would not have ever gotten into the position to save Israel from the famine that eventually came. My heart shudders at the thought of how many people may have compromised in their walk with God and never amounted to anything more than the mediocre. They took bribes, succumbed to peer pressure for sex, drugs, corruption, and what have you. And now they have big mansions but never became the president of the nation; now they're the Head of Marketing but they could have been the CEO.

His promises and eternal reward for Joseph would have died in his pants or on his laps had the young man succumbed to that evil temptation. This is why you must never think of anything as just a little sin that doesn't not mean much, because that is not true. A little leaven leaveneth the entire lump – if it is corruption, it will seep into everything that is you and yours and contaminate it all.

If Joseph had slept with that woman, he may

or may not have still gone to prison – even though his going to prison would have been justified – but it is possible he may never have learnt eventually how to interpret dreams. Certainly, the chance of him being the given that mighty office later would have been significantly diminished in the face of his sin.

When Mrs. Potiphar reported the issue, she did not call his name, "Joseph." She said it was "that Hebrew boy" (Genesis 39:14). It is at moments like this that you realize it was never just about Joseph but about the entire nation of Israel which he represented. You want to remember that too – it is not just about you but about the kingdom which you claim to be part of, the kingdom of God. So, stand up for what is right, represent Him well, and win the crown, not just for you but for heaven.

Chapter 20

INTELLIGENCE AND ABILITIES

Your God-given graces are meant to be used and perfected. We often hear of people saying things like, you are not a blessing until you can bless other people, and it is true. You have nothing in this world except what you have been given. When you arrived here on earth, you had absolutely nothing on you, and when you leave this world, regardless of what your contemporaries adorn your body with when they want to bury you, you are not taking a single stitch of it to the world beyond. Every. Single. Thing. You. Have. Had. And. Owned. between your cradle and your grave, you have had because God permitted you to have it.

It does not matter if you are the most hardworking person on the planet or if you were born to the wealthiest family that ever lived. All that you have, you have because God permitted you to have it. Jesus reminded

Pontius Pilate of it just as He was about to be sentenced to death: "Thou couldest have no power at all against me, except it were given thee from above..." (John 19:11). It helps to remember these things so that we all can stay humble.

Yes, even folks who are wicked and cruel; even leaders who abuse their offices and usurp the resources of their people – they are all there because God allowed it to be so. Hence, we come to understand that our being blessed is not about how smart we are, how wonderfully positioned, or how fortunate we have been. It was just God who was showing Himself God. We honour Him for this, and then we dish it out freely so that it doesn't canker in our hands.

> *"Heal the sick, cleanse the lepers, raise the dead, cast out devils: freely ye have received, freely give."*
> -   *Matthew 10:8*

What you have was given to you; give it back out. Everybody, does not matter your status in life, is given something for the benefit of the whole body – the entire world. And if you are thinking that having all that you have and canning it is the proof of your being blessed, then you need to watch out because very soon, you will start stinking and rotting away. It's called stagnancy, and you were never designed for that! Every good river gives out – it is flowed into by streams and springs, and then it feeds out into bigger rivers, and eventually the ocean. If it does not do this, things die in it and it begins to smell. Like the Dead Sea out there by the Mediterranean, you can tell the instant you see it that something is not right.

It's out there for everyone to see. Some of the wealthiest people on the planet suffer from some of the most debilitating diseases known to mankind – ulcers, cancers, heart and blood diseases, kidney complications... it is a terrible list. You look at them and wonder how they got so sick while having so much, and you don't immediately understand that sometimes people get that ill because they are holding on to things that they are supposed to let go of. You look at the simple folks and you find them happy and thriving despite their condition, disease far from many of them, and you don't get that sometimes "Better is little with the fear of God..." (Proverbs 15:16).

> *"But unto every one of us is given grace according to the measure of the gift of Christ. Wherefore he saith, When he ascended up on high, he led captivity captive, and gave gifts unto men. (Now that he ascended, what is it but that he also descended first into the lower parts of the earth? He that descended is the same also that ascended up far above all heavens, that he might fill all things.) And he gave some, apostles; and some, prophets; and some, evangelists; and some, pastors and teachers; For the perfecting of the saints, for the work of the ministry, for the edifying of the body of Christ: Till we all come in the unity of the faith, and of the knowledge of the Son of God, unto a perfect man, unto*

281

*the measure of the stature of
the fullness of Christ:"*
-        *Ephesians 4:7-13*

Every one of us is given grace, however much
or little, to profit to the benefit of all. Your
intelligence and abilities must be used for the
service of others.

Joseph had that gift of dreams and
interpretation, and he had no doubt about it.
He used it in and out of the prison. I try to
imagine what could have been if he refused to
use it in the prison. Perhaps he could have felt
like he was merely depriving the baker and the
butler, and nobody would have benefitted
from it. Except that, in the long run, it turned
out that he was only helping himself by being
a blessing to his brothers in incarceration!

Oh, there would have been confusion and
anarchy all over the country of Egypt when
there was no one to interpret the king's dream.
There would have been no preparation for the
famine during the years of plenty. The future
they were to create and preserve in Egypt, the
one which involved the Israelites all shipping
in at that time to save their generations may

have been twisted somehow or another... Or possibly, God could have discarded him and done it with someone else because Joseph was too proud in his gifting to surrender and allow himself to be used.

Talents are meant to be used, and when they are not used they can be taken away. The story of the talents comes readily to mind here as we recall that the slothful servant was stripped of his one good talent, which was given to the more productive steward with 10 talents, while he was cast into a place of weeping and gnashing of teeth. The servant had felt that since he had only one and there was little he could do with it, the thing to do would be to hide his talent. Obviously, he was mistaken on that one.

The master returned, commended those who had traded with their talents, and punished him. See, our lives become worse off when we refuse to serve God with our gifts and talents. We are taught in Exodus 23:25 that if we serve him, he will bless our bread and our water and take sickness away from us. We have got to know that God also means the exact opposite, which is that, if we refuse to serve Him, He will not bless our bread and our water, and He will not be taking those sicknesses and diseases away from our midst. When one tries to imagine how many diseases the devil has in store out there for those that he is allowed to inflict with them, one can understand how catastrophic it would be to be at his mercy. Certainly, no child of God needs to be there.

We must serve Christ and serve others so that God will in turn, turn around and bless us. We must never allow other people's comments and our own comforts to hinder us from going to all the way in the service of God and mankind using all that we have at our disposal. It doesn't matter what precisely it is – physical, mental, spiritual, financial... Remember, we all have different abilities. Find yours and excel with it.

Chapter 21

A NAME

To make a name for yourself is to become prominent or well known; basically, to achieve distinction. In spite of the suffering of Joseph, he achieved distinction both in the house of Potiphar and later in the prison. Little wonder it came instantaneously when he finally showed up in the palace. It is because it became a habit for him – distinction; and to this day it is associated with his name everywhere that he is mentioned.

A name it is. We hear names like George Washington, William Shakespeare, Warren Buffet, Kenneth Hagin, and Billy Graham, and we never have to wonder what it is that they do or what they stand or stood for. Their names always ring a bell because they stood for distinction in their spheres of endeavour. Joseph also became the name around the world in his own time because he stood for distinction too everywhere that he was. Yet it started with a simple dream back in his daddy's tents, until it evolved into the interpretation of dreams for the lowly in the prison, and finally high up there in the palace, he was standing before one of the most powerful men in the world and he was interpreting dreams.

Sure, a man's gift will make room for him, as the Bible says. Your gift will make room for you as it did for Mr. Joseph. Only do not bury it in obscurity, but diligently push it to distinction.

"Then Pharaoh said to joseph, 'In my dream I was standing on the bank of the Nile. When out of the river there came up seven cows, fat and sleek, and they grazed among the reeds. After them, seven other cows came up- scrawny and very ugly cows in all the land of Egypt. The lean, ugly cows ate up the seven fat cows that came up first. But even after they ate them, no one could tell that

they had done so; they looked just as ugly as before then I woke up. In my dream I saw seven ears of corn, full and good, growing on a single stalk. After them, seven other ears sprouted- withered and thin and scorched by the east wind. The thin ears of corn swallowed up the seven good ears. I told this to the magicians, but none of them could explain it to me. Then joseph said to pharaoh, 'The dreams of pharaoh are one and the same. God has revealed to pharaoh what he is about to do. The seven good cows are seven years; it is one and the same dream. The seven lean, ugly cows that came up afterwards are seven years, and so are the seven worthless ears of corn scorched by the east wind: they are seven years of famine.''

\- *Genesis 41:17-27.*

He listened to pharaoh and predicted seven years of feasting to be followed by seven years of famine. Joseph's diligence was eventually met by God's grace and the opportunity in a meeting to show what cloth he was cut from.

And this is another important matter. You cannot – must not – fall into the place of opportunity coming for you and you are found wanting. This must never happen to any of us. We must be ready at all times – be instant, in season, out of season. No man knows the day nor the hour when [God/opportunity/breakthrough] will show up, so we cannot sit on our hands doing nothing. We must continue to hone our craft, getting better and better always, until one day someone or something shows up and catapults us into superstardom.

All Joseph did was interpret the dream of pharaoh and the king was flabbergasted enough that he wondered where such a man with the spirit of God came from. He did not even consider that this man had been in prison and/or a slave for the greater part of thirteen years. It did not matter that the man was only thirty years old and perhaps still had the smell of the dungeons about him. He saw the excellence of a man who leaned on God for his supply but would still not hold his hand from good effort in building up others. He saw someone who also could do the work of preserving the food for the famine of seven years inside this great man of wisdom. He barely took a moment to think of it.

> *"The plan seemed good to Pharaoh and to all his officials. So Pharaoh asked them, 'can we find anyone like this man, one in whom is the spirit of God? Then Pharaoh said to Joseph, 'Since God has made all this known to you, there is no one so discerning and wise as you. You shall be in charge of the palace, and all my people are to submit to your orders. Only with respect to throne will I be greater than you. So Pharaoh said to Joseph, 'I hereby put you in charge of the whole land of Egypt. Then Pharaoh took his signet ring from his finger and*

put it on Joseph's finger. He dressed him in robes of fine linen and put a gold chain round his neck. He made him ride in a chariot as his second –in-command, and people shouted before him, 'Make way! Thus he put him in charge of the whole land of Egypt. Then Pharaoh said to Joseph, 'I am Pharaoh, but without your word no one will lift hand or foot in all Egypt'. Pharaoh gave Joseph the name Zaphenant-Paneah and gave him Asenath daughter of Potiphera, priest of On, to be his wife. And joseph went throughout the land of Egypt."
-        *Genesis 41:37-45*

Automatically, the office of the Minister for Food and Agriculture opened up and went right to Joseph, and with it came all the paraphernalia of a king's office. Joseph received the king's signet, a gold necklace, fine clothes, a new (Egyptian) name – Zaphenant-Paneah – and a wife, Asenath. The people could not match him for the grace of God. There was no objection, it was a question of life and death. They needed him and the grace that he carried.

Little wonder there's a saying that "your dream is the reason for the way you are!" It certainly stands to reason; it is who you are. It is what has given you a sense of meaning and purpose; it is what drives you into your chosen future; it is what gives the meaning to your life. And inevitably, it speaks because you have been patiently and diligently working at it even in the ignominy of forgetfulness.

Finally, it was the time of his manifestation, and it spoke.

May you not be found wanting when it is your time?

Joseph created the Agricultural policy and infrastructure of Egypt in those days, facilitating new ways to manage resources that the people simply had never thought of before. All his policies worked too, and he was able to carry the nation, and perhaps half the then-known world, through the famine and rescue his own family in the process. His dream came to pass.

A lot of people have dared to dream like he did. Sir Isaac Newton discovered the theory of gravity. This body of knowledge that he discovered affected the whole world so positively that by the time he died in 1772 at the age of 88, his pall was borne by three earls, two dukes and the Lord Chancellor. He was buried as a king who had done well for his subjects. Beloved, DARE TO DREAM.

Part 5

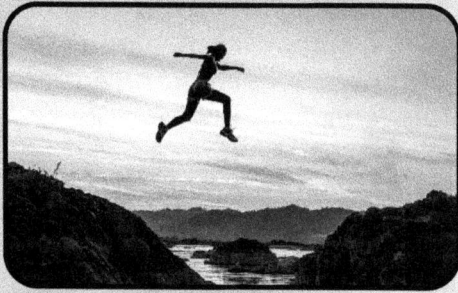

IF I PERISH,
I PERISH!

THE PALACE PARTY

"Now it came to pass in the days of Ahasuerus, (this is Ahasuerus which reigned, from India even unto Ethiopia, over an hundred and seven and twenty provinces:) That in those days, when the king Ahasuerus sat on the throne of his kingdom, which was in Shushan the palace, In the third year of his reign, he made a feast unto all his princes and his servants; the power of Persia and Media, the nobles and princes of the provinces, being before him: When he showed the riches of his glorious kingdom and the honour of his excellent majesty many days, even an hundred and fourscore days."

-   Esther 1:1-4

The Jews had been carted out of their own home country for about seventy years, and at this point in the story they were exiled in Persia, the vast pagan empire that ruled over most of the then known world. It was a rough time for people of the faith in a faraway land, but they had made a life for themselves, and some had even begun returning to their homeland. The people grew more in number, and despite being under punishment, God was still with them. This was not something they had planned or wanted – they would have loved to be in their fatherland but strictly speaking they had brought this upon themselves and now life had to go on. So, those still in exile lived with the hope that they would return to their land someday according to God's initial promise.

The psalmist said concerning himself that failure to believe God was failure in and of itself. Specifically, he would have failed if he had not believed God; and this was true too of these children of God who lived in diaspora in Persian times, and of any human being anywhere, really. A child of God does not have a choice but to keep hoping in the Lord. Anybody who fails to heed the Word of God

295

or believe in it totally is bound to fail inevitably, even if they think things are great, and even if the rot and decay is not immediately apparent.

Hebrews 10:35, 38 says "So do not throw away your confidence; it will be richly rewarded.

But my righteous one will live by faith, and if he shrinks back, I will not be pleased with him."Keen words from the Good Book. God is not happy at all with those who do not believe in Him. As a matter of fact, it is your belief – your faith – in Him which acts as your currency to receive anything from Him at all. "For without faith it is impossible to please God!"

No matter what circumstance we find ourselves in, we must make the effort to grow and increase because that mandate, that grace, is made available to us from the beginning. "Be fruitful and multiply,"our God instructs, and that life was born immediately within us simply because God said so. So, even in the dunghill or deepest dungeon, we can be fruitful, and so were the Jews in diaspora in that day. Mordecai, Esther's uncle turned out

296

to be the leader of the Jews in that region and had brought her up as a single parent but with the right tenets instilled in her. No, we never get the whole picture of the household of Mordecai, but it was always he and his cousin Hadassah – a Hebrew name which means 'evergreen' shrub.

Imagine being on exile, two parents gone, unmarried uncle as the parent, and now she has to obey this man because she had no other choice? This made Esther the young lady of the house, carrying the load of all feminine activities for that family. Cooking, cleaning, and managing the insecurities of others, especially with many young Jewish boys all around the place...This girl had to have her head on right, or she would go wrong.

Destiny under fire; this young woman of courage and humility was a brand all on her own! Her Persian name meant Star – something she would eventually become as wife of King Ahasuerus, and as deliverer of the Jews.
The End of the Vashti Era.

"On the seventh day, when the

heart of the king was merry with wine, he commanded Mehuman, Biztha, Harbona, Bigtha, and Abagtha, Zethar, and Carcas, the seven chamberlains that served in the presence of Ahasuerus the king, to bring Vashti the queen before the king with the crown royal, to show the people and the princes her beauty: for she was fair to look on. But the queen Vashti refused to come at the king's commandment by his chamberlains: therefore was the king very wroth, and his anger burned in him. Then the king said to the wise men, which knew the times, (for so was the king's manner toward all that knew law and judgment: And the next unto him was Carshena, Shethar, Admatha, Tarshish, Meres, Marsena, and Memucan, the seven princes of Persia and Media, which saw the king's face, and which sat the first in

298

the kingdom;) What shall we do unto the queen Vashti according to law, because she hath not performed the commandment of the king A h a s u e r u s b y t h e chamberlains? And Memucan answered before the king and the princes, Vashti the queen hath not done wrong to the king only, but also to all the princes, and to all the people that are in all the provinces of the king Ahasuerus. For this deed of the queen shall come abroad unto all women, so that they shall despise their husbands in their eyes, when it shall be reported, The king Ahasuerus commanded Vashti the queen to be brought in before him, but she came not. Likewise shall the ladies of Persia and Media say this day unto all the king's princes, which have heard of the deed of the queen. Thus shall there arise too much contempt and

299

wrath. If it please the king, let there go a royal commandment from him, and let it be written among the laws of the Persians and the Medes, that it be not altered, That Vashti come no more before king Ahasuerus; and let the king give her royal estate unto another that is better than she. And when the king's decree which he shall make shall be published throughout all his empire, (for it is great,) all the wives shall give to their husbands honour, both to great and small. And the saying pleased the king and the princes; and the king did according to the word of Memucan: For he sent letters into all the king's provinces, into every province according to the writing thereof, and to every people after their language, that every man should bear rule in his own house, and that it should be published according to the

300

language of every people."
-        *Esther 1:10-*

King Ahasuerus had just ended a party which lasted the greater part of six months, during which he showed off his splendor to…everyone. Then his very beautiful wife had to go and pull a complicated one and sour his merry mood by failing to show up when she was bid.

I have heard preachers say that the King was being unfair to his queen by demanding she come show herself off to his subjects, like an objectifiable piece of meat. He really did have to be drunk to be that inconsiderate to the woman who supposedly completed him. I see another point of view though, which is that she held the glory of the King and the kingdom. She had the beauty and the opportunity to put on display that which she was richly endowed with for the honor of her husband, king and Kingdom and to refuse this privilege is to deny her unique place and relevance. She refused her moment in the limelight and thereby triggered darkness while consigning herself to disposable and forgettable history. The woman was created to be adaptable helper to the man and to that extent, she is the glory of the man. She is his helper and whatever that help translated into, that is what she is meant to be. Vashti forgot to remember this. And true, she probably remained a beautiful woman for the rest of her days but:

a) She ceased to be queen;
b) She ceased to come before the man she was intended to help and complete; and
c) She ceased to be relevant – simply.

We read no more about Vashti for the rest of the Bible. She sunk her future, her marriage, her relevance… all over a moment of pride and rebellion. Reflective really of many situations seen in the world today – homes breaking, men running away, wives running away, Christians compromising, society capitulating. It is a genuine apostasy in which those who know their God need to be doubly sober and vigilant, understanding that the days are evil and that we all need an extra cruse of grace to wade through.

Vashti's fall is Esther's Opportunity

At the point Esther comes into the picture,

Vashti had just been dethroned and was no longer 'queen'. That talk of town on the lips of young and old was unprecedented in the history of the empire, and it took acute deliberation by the king's advisers to design a swift and workable solution. Vashti's audacity to turn down the King was cause for practically worldwide concern! She must have been on that throne a long time, possibly an older woman by now, to have developed a level of contempt or apathy for the office.

In marriage, a man and woman leave and cleave to each other, and the man becomes head of the family. Apologists try to explain this away, but it is precisely what the Bible says it is. The wise husband listens to his wife's opinion over issues, but the last say belongs to him. He is called to be leader in his home but this is more than just authority; this is a grave responsibility for which he must answer, so he does this in the fear of God, giving regard to his wife and understanding that each choice could bear beautiful or dire consequences for the people in his care.

That is the government of God in place, and it was not ordained by man. We can try all we can to be politically correct or to keep up with

303

the times, but God's mandate has always been His mandate from the day He spoke the words unto… eternity.I cannot over flog the fact that the queen had an obligation to the King, irrespective of what the general public had to think or say about the situation – and this, whether the man's heart was merry or not.

Vashti was definitely both influential and powerful, enough to be able to throw her own party for the women while her husband was likewise making merry. So, when she did this rebellion thing, her case became a government issue too. See, because of her position, the choice she made – while she may have seen it only as a personal one – was going to have deep-seated ramifications, not only for herself, but for the entire kingdom.

Children of God, in all our getting, we must get both wisdom and understanding. Whatever choice you make with your life is never only just about your life. We get this thing in the movies and television these days, about how "It's my life and I will live it as I want to", or "I can do whatever I want to with my body" … All of these are terribly wrong notions. You did not make yourself; you do

304

not own yourself – it's not just your life any more. Especially if you already have Christ in your life (or should I say, if Christ already has you), you must remember what the Bible says:

> *"What? know ye not that your body is the temple of the Holy Ghost which is in you, which ye have of God, and ye are not your own? For ye are bought with a price: therefore glorify God in your body, and in your spirit, which are God's."*
> -   *1 Corinthians 6:19-20*

You cannot just go into a husband's life and act like you like – no ma! You go in there and act like God expects you to act; like God made you to act. The same goes for the man – you're there to represent God to that woman, not just to bounce her around like you like. There are people watching you, people whom God wants to use your life to brag about. You don't want to let God down.

It is written in black-and-white in scripture. In Ephesians 5:25-30 we learn of Jesus working to ensure that His bride, the Church, is

305

cleansed through the water of the Word in order for her to be presented to Himself, and of course to His Father. Two chapters earlier in Ephesians 3:9-12, we learn that God had purposed since eternity to show off His wisdom to all "the principalities and powers in heavenly places" through what He is able to do in and with the Church.

See, God (the head) has always been about showing off Himself (His body/the Church) to those around Him. Seeing He made man in His own image, is it so farfetched that a man would want to show off his wife? Is there any man on the planet who doesn't want to feel a sense of pride over his own achievement when other men look at his wife? The woman after all IS the glory of the man (1 Corinthians 11:7) – his crown (Proverbs 12:4). You put a crown on your head to affirm who you are – a king. When the crown refuses to come on your head, it's kind of no good anymore: salt that has lost its savor; it gets to be cast out into the streets and trodden underfoot by men. The sum of what am saying here is this; woman, use all your God given power, beauty and potential capabilities to support and complement your husband. It is not

306

demeaning but rather, it is your privilege and also a thing of power! Likewise, real men should deploy everything in their power to honor and defend their own wives even at the cost of their very lives; this is proper and it's the Bible standard for marriage.

Unfortunately, Vashti lost out and sadly, it happens to too many other women in marriages all over the world today. The fact that there are women who still strut their stuff and flaunt their broken homes in the name of independence and feminism all over social media and television does not make it any less appalling. It is something that can and should be addressed at home and in the Church, so that at least a few can be saved who will influence the world in a positive way going forward, young ones who will be light to the world and speak with the enemy at the gate. O how I wish you and I will be those few people who would salt the earth with our commitment to doing it God's way.

Sadly for Vashti, this was not an incident that took place in the bedroom but one which took place in public. The royal advisers had to come into the picture to stem a potentially

307

deadly avalanche of women misbehaving in their homes. Had this been present day, it would have been all over the papers, the internet, and social media, much like a recent appalling story of a monarch whose wife decided to leave her recently crowned husband for... whatever.

Ridicule the monarch and the monarchy is what Vashti did, dragging his authority in the mud practically in front of the entire comity of nations. A lot of people may be numbed to the implications of that in present day because it is so common, but even back then, perhaps a thousand years before Jesus was born, the wise ones among the people could immediately see the far-reaching implications of what had been done – how several homes, families, marriages, and the society at large could be affected by it. Little question, those in the parliament who had one thing or the other against her were going to have a field day now because she had blown it big time. She was not going to escape judgment.

The mistakes Christians make these days are literally alarming, especially with respect to living lives of victory. God loves us and covers our behinds all the time, but all too often we would venture off on our own and break hedges around us which are supposed to protect us. The man being the head of a woman means that he was meant to "cover her head" at all times, meaning she was supposed to do everything in her power to make her head look good, to protect him from ridicule. Yes, even if it meant moments of discomfort for her! Endure it for the sake of what is important so that no one would find occasion to hold anything against you.

But here she served herself up in a platter. And boy, did the sharks come swimming!
"She gotta go!" The disciplinary committee sat many times. The mighty queen was brought down. One day she was the high and revered queen of the most powerful and influential man on the planet, and the next day she was "Auntie". (Title gone)

Call it fear or what have you, but the kingdom could ill afford the ripples of repercussions that her actions were to have on the society. Wives would see that since the king didn't get respect in his own house, they didn't need to give respect to their own husbands anymore.

A statement had to be made. Queen Vashti was dethroned.

There are those who would say today that it is overrated and overstated, but if the Bible says it once, or it says it half a dozen times: every woman who is married must learn one little something, and that thing is called submission. You don't like it, go take it up with God.

Ephesians 5:21-29 says:

> *Submitting yourselves one to another in the fear of God. Wives, submit yourselves unto your own husbands, as unto the Lord. For the husband is the head of the wife, even as Christ is the head of the church: and he is the savior of the body. Therefore as the church is subject unto Christ, so let the wives be to their own husbands in everything. Husbands, love your wives, even as Christ also loved the church, and gave himself for it; That he might sanctify and*

310

cleanse it with the washing of water by the word, That he might present it to himself a glorious church, not having spot, or wrinkle, or any such thing; but that it should be holy and without blemish. So ought men to love their wives as their own bodies. He that loveth his wife loveth himself. For no man ever yet hated hisown flesh; but nourisheth and cherisheth it, even as the Lord the church:

The thing is not even as difficult as it sounds, especially when done in an atmosphere of love and understanding, under the covering of God's love. Bickering, complaining, nagging, sulking, pouting, anger, lashing out, disobedience... even being sassy, sexy, or seductive – these things will not work in the long run; wives will win through submission to their husbands. It is part of the winning process of a fulfilled life of a married woman. Many imagine they will simply remarry if their marriage does not work out, but God has a way of continuously bringing you back to face the same problems you think you ran away from. Simply, you always meet the word like a stumbling block before you even if you go through the tenth marriage because you have refused to allow it to enter and change you.

The sooner you submit under God, the sooner you win and fulfill purpose in your life and marriage. Let us learn to do it God's way and honestly victory in all areas of our lives will follow sooner than we imagine. If we don't, this isn't a curse – we could very well end up like Vashti: shamed, discarded, and forgotten. Within reason, we can be sure she could never marry again. She had failed the trial! (According to the culture of that day. Who wants to marry the dethroned Queen?

Chapter 23

ESTHER, FAVORED, VICTORIOUS
AND ON FIRE

"I returned, and saw under the sun, that the race is not to the swift, nor the battle to the strong, neither yet bread to the wise, nor yet riches to men of understanding, nor yet favor to men of skill; but time and chance happeneth to them all."   *- Ecclesiastes 9:11*

The fall of Queen Vashti created the opportunity for Esther to fulfill her prophetic destiny. Who is now Esther to take the place of a queen? Esther must have wondered why all this trouble. Like Mary Mother of Jesus, a woman, quiet, humble, and close to God's heart, was going about her business and would have loved to maintain that quiet and peaceable life, but all of a sudden she was pointed out by God to be a special woman. The pressure she had to go through to fulfill the destiny of being a mother to Jesus. Same with Esther, she would have loved to remain on her own and by herself, protected, neglected, unremarkable, married to some young Jew or other at some point. Except God saw her differently.

I imagine the butterflies in her stomach when Uncle Mordecai instructed her to go for the King's pageant when he was looking for a new wife to replace the deposed Vashti. Esther would have thought it impossible that she could be selected for the position, stranger in a strange land that she was. She was not to disclose her identity, but what if someone found out in there and reported to the king's keeper of the women, Hegai? No pressure!

Then there were the rules and implications. If she wasn't picked she would become a concubine of the king for the rest of her life. If she was, she would belong to this older man for the rest of her life – did she want that?
No pressure.

---

*Did she possess what it took -
the qualities and attributes
that would make the Queen of
Persia – the stately carriage,
the queenly disposition, the
graceful attitude, and the
ability to converse, convince,
and carry people along?*

How was she ever going to earn the respect,
entertain, or play the role Vashti had failed to
play? What chances did a slave girl, an
orphan, stand in filling the shoes of another
who had probably been prepared for the role
all her life and had still failed at it? Now she
was being asked to command an entourage in
the Kings palace.

No pressure.

*"Trust in the LORD, and do
good; so shalt thou dwell in the
land, and verily thou shalt be
fed. Delight thyself also in the
LORD; and he shall give thee
the desires of thine heart.
Commit thy way unto the
LORD; trust also in him; and*

315

he shall bring it to pass. And he shall bring forth thy righteousness as the light, and thy judgment as the noonday."
-        *Psalm 37:3-6*

Esther's destiny was not something coming on a bed of roses, but one that was being pushed in a big heated oven, under fire. She hadn't even had a say in the matter. She'd been brought up to obey her big cousin Mordecai, so all of this was really kind of just happening to her. So, heart-in-mouth, she simply went on ahead in obedience and submission.

This is another important matter that has been taken for granted in present day, but one which God does not take lightly at all. This is not about stating rules to put us all back under the law, but about understanding how God thinks and what is precious to Him, particularly with respect to a passage like Jeremiah 9:23-24, which essentially intimates that the important thing in life is understanding and knowing God, as well as the things that are important to Him.

A woman unmarried belongs to her father (or

father-figure in her life) until the day that she does get married, after which she belongs to her husband. Rebellion against the will of 'Daddy' is not acceptable in God's book – whether you like it or not, whether 'Daddy' is doing well or not, is not really your business, Lady. Your business is to bring honor to your daddy through your obedience.

Statements such as "this is my life and I will live it like I want", do not have a place of real value in God's kingdom. If Daddy don't like the man you want to marry, you want to go to Daddy and work it out with him first before you go on ahead with that marriage, or else you are not going to get Daddy's blessing, a powerful thing spiritually.

Esther had never met the king in person before, and she had every reason to be concerned that he might not even be the kind of man she had prayed for. Perhaps she could see that he was tall, dark, and handsome from his likeness across Shushan the Palace and other far reaches of the empire he may have visited; but was he caring, sensitive, understanding, and romantic? There was no way she could know this aforetime. The man

317

had fired his last wife, for crying out loud. Would he do the same to her? Did he have a sense of humor, like she imagined her husband would have? Did he know how to take care of a woman, or was he the kind who believed he was God-sent to women – that she was lucky to be married to him?
Questions!

Esther didn't have answers as she was placed under Hegai the Eunuch and keeper of the king's women. All she had was character built in the furnace of submission to a God-fearing uncle, and now a destiny being further forged in the fires of obedience. And inevitably, her good character started to show forth. In the king's harem, away from home, she gravitated toward the sage wisdom of the older man and obeyed Hegai. Another note of warning to all young up-and-comers, this young lady didn't act like she knew what it was all about; instead she did all she was asked to do and as a result found favor.

Folks, there is a favor that comes with not undermining authority. It is from God, yes, but it is often channeled through the person whom you are showing regard to. This goes to everyone in every walk of life – worker in church, janitor in an office, secretary, …If you show regard and deference to those who are superior to you, they tend to become nicer and give you tips to get you further ahead in life. Proverbs 16:20 says "whoever gives heed to instruction prospers, and blessed is he who trusts in the Lord."

Child of God, obedience to God's word and instruction is key to success and prosperity if we are going to walk with Him. Romans 5:19 acts as both an example and instruction in this regard:

> *"For as by one man's disobedience many were made sinners, so by the obedience of one shall many be made righteous. Moreover the law entered, that the offence might abound. But where sin abounded, grace did much more abound: That as sin hath reigned unto death, even so might grace reign through righteousness unto eternal life by Jesus Christ our Lord."*
> -   *Romans 5:19-21*

Esther in this story typifies Jesus the Savior of the whole world. If Jesus had chickened out of the whole plan when the heat was turned on him, what would have become of humanity? There would have been no redemption for man, or it would have taken some other thousands of years! But thank God for her obedience; Esther did not understand why she had to go through the awkward and harrowing process, but submitted in obedience to her father, Mordecai.

Understandably as the days grew closer, she would grow more concerned. The King was going to be spending a night each with each of the girls, and by morning might decide never to see them again. There had to be scores of them – hundreds, maybe. Was this a show of power or of tradition, choosing a bride exclusively by beauty and sexual prowess? It was degrading, yet there was no getting out of it – no going back to her family and loved ones. In short, there was to be no hope for the future beyond this one assignment!

Perhaps the closest thing we have to this in the 21st century is the story of Sindiswa Dlamini, who was said to have been spotted by a 45-

year-old Monarch as she and thousands of other Swazi maidens danced bare breasted before him. She was only 18 years old at the time and had just finished secondary school a year earlier!

(The Telegraph News from Africa. 12th October 2017).

Fight the good fight of faith
The whole point of this story is not to suggest a prescription of primordial regressive roles for womanhood but on the contrary, to shine the light on a true path of honor that all women called by God to be movers and shakers can proudly emulate.

Psalm 44:5 says

> **"Through you we push back our enemies; through your name we trample our foes."**

There are times we go through challenges that are genuinely bigger than we are and we simply must trust God to help us while we are in them. We need to remember always that it is never over on this side of heaven. As we win on one stage, we typically run right into another level of challenge in the very next

321

instant, each one stretching us a little further than the last. Our hope must remain in God for His thoughts for us are of good and not of evil to give us an expected end.

For young Hadassah, the pressure was only just beginning. She would go through the harrowing preparation and selection process. She would miraculously get picked among the numerous girls at the palace from across Shushan and its regions. Then she would finally get married to the man she did not really know to spend the rest of her days as his 'companion' and 'help-meet'.

Not to mention, getting married to someone merely gives you the liberty to live with this person. It does not reveal the troubles to be expected or how they will come. It by no means implies that everything will be rosy from that point on. In fact, quite the contrary, it is promised that there will be such situations once we get married that some will wish to disengage. But there is nothing children of God go through that is not known to God, if not even carefully managed by Him. He knows these things before they happen, and He preempts them in favor of His own.

A young Christian woman was married to her dashing lover and was so happy God had met all her desires: they were to be happily married ever after. However, while they were on the way home from their honeymoon, and only a few kilometers/miles to their base, it happened – the course of their lives was to be altered forever. The handsome sportsman's leg had to be amputated as a consequence of the ghastly accident, and his beautiful bride needed to become the legs for her husband. Talk about pressure! The experience almost ended her. It without doubt put her 'in sickness and in health" vows to test.

Thankfully, our lady stuck through so that they are still married today.

Favor shone down on Esther and she was soon the envy of every female in the kingdom and toast of every Jewish heart. It was a costly elevation because it required her total commitment to this assignment and there was no going back.

There is an African saying which goes 'the bigger the head, the bigger the headache,' which rings true in this situation. Being a queen is a whole new demanding assignment – one which gave her women to oversee, dire situations to deal with, and a husband who could go months without even asking after her. Taking charge of maidens in the palace was hard work; learning palace ethics was pressure; and she couldn't just walk into her husband's room any time she felt like it, even though he was her lover. Protocols strictly observed.

God has other plans – Wrap your head round it!

As if time had been waiting for her to sit on the throne, trouble came. Mordecai had to be the man about town since he was heading the Jews and was their spokesperson. God's faithfulness to His children revealed the plan Haman – and enemy of God's people – had incubated and waited for just the right time to execute: to exterminate the Jews. The plan had been fully hatched, and the man was in position to manipulate it into existence, having recently been promoted to that place of swaying influence.

Role model Mordecai mourned but it was time to act; Esther had matured in the palace and held a sway all her own, even though she did not know it yet. Mordecai approached to let her know the problem and what was required of her in that moment, and like most of us, when the dire straits of our situation look us right in the face, she balked a little... until Mordecai sent her that strong reminder:

> *"...Think not with thyself that thou shalt escape in the king's house, more than all the Jews. For if thou altogether holdest thy peace at this time, then shall there enlargement and deliverance arise to the Jews from another place; but thou and thy father's house shall be destroyed: and who knoweth whether thou art come to the kingdom for such a time as this?" Esther 4:13-14. Boy did she need those words. She gained some confidence immediately, mixed with determination and resolve. She was going to act, even if it cost her... everything.*

Queen Esther Risks all her gain, saying, If I perish, I Perish!

325

Confidence, self-assurance, feelings of certainty, the quality of trusting. Now she was queen and the battle had changed from mere survival to actually putting her own neck on the line for her entire race. Suddenly it was fiercer, the challenges steeper, but she was not going to be pushed around anymore because now she understood her purpose.

Too many of us accept anything life dumps on us just like that; even though we are God's children, we lack confidence in God and often we don't just push back when the devil throws stuff at us. There is no doubt the need to stand our ground and claim all the victories that God has given, but when we don't know this, or when we allow fear and trepidation to paralyze us, we can end up being on the same spot forever, unprogressive and unproductive; or worse, we can end up being bowled over by something we could have overcome by taking a stand.

The devil can have breakfast on anyone's heads while the individual looks on expecting something to happen. You never become a hero if you never push back. Finally, Esther understood this, pushed, and won!

Life is by no means a walk in the park, but lying there and taking it in the face again and again will not get you anywhere fast. Life does not usually give you what you want on a platter of gold - it makes you work for it. Little wonder the Bible teaches that: "Since the days of John the Baptist, the kingdom of God suffers violence, and the violent take it by force."

Yes, the kingdom of heaven has pressures too. The pressure to excel, the pressure to please God by putting in a little more than your ordinary. Esther knew she had to do something, but she understood also that she had to do it on her own terms else she would be done in by it. She could not walk right up to the king even though she was under pressure – that would cost her life needlessly, and the matter at hand would not even be addressed. With grace she stayed calm, took time to think, and then strategies for optimal action. Unlike the three Hebrew brothers who took the immediate decision to be "not careful" to answer the king over the matter of the golden image (Daniel 3:16-18), Esther took the scenic route, the way of femininity, the soft power if you like.

327

Folks, you are not who you are by fluke, and you are never wherever you find yourself by mistake. If you are a woman, it is because there is something uniquely you that is pertinent to where you find yourself that will either solve the matter at hand, or that will contribute significantly to resolving the situation. If you are a wife – never mind that your husband is Mr. Nice Guy or the Grinch – you are in that man's life to achieve a purpose that has something to do with you being a woman. You don't need to get stuck up in "how I wish I had been a man"; that kind of thinking will paralyze you from acting.

Sir, as a man you need to believe that there are certain doors that will open to a woman which will never open to you. Respect that crucial little detail about the woman you call wife and give her room to excel at who she is. You could be a slave-boy in Potiphar's house, a young slave-girl in Naaman's family, or a widow in a small town named Zarephath – God uses our disposition the way it is, and always glorifies Himself. A hot person is backed by the Holy Spirit every bit as much as a gentle team player, or a child in your home. Just because he is an usher in the Church does

328

not imply that he has a lesser support from God than the pastor on the pulpit.

"When Mordecai perceived all that was done, Mordecai rent his clothes, and put on sackcloth with ashes, and went out into the midst of the city, and cried with a loud and a bitter cry; And came even before the king's gate: for none might enter into the king's gate clothed with sackcloth. And in every province, whithersoever the king's commandment and his decree came, there was great mourning among the Jews, and fasting, and weeping, and wailing; and many lay in sackcloth and ashes. So Esther's maids and her chamberlains came and told it her. Then was the queen exceedingly grieved; and she sent raiment to clothe Mordecai, and to take away his sackcloth from him: but he received it not. Then called

Esther for Hatach, one of the king's chamberlains, whom he had appointed to attend upon her, and gave him a commandment to Mordecai, to know what it was, and why it was. So Hatach went forth to Mordecai unto the street of the city, which was before the king's gate. And Mordecai told him of all that had happened unto him, and of the sum of the money that Haman had promised to pay to the king's treasuries for the Jews, to destroy them. Also he gave him the copy of the writing of the decree that was given at Shushan to destroy them, to show it unto Esther, and to declare it unto her, and to charge her that she should go in unto the king, to make supplication unto him, and to make request before him for her people. And Hatach came and told Esther the words of Mordecai. Again Esther spake

330

unto Hatach, and gave him c o m m a n d m e n t   u n t o Mordecai; All the king's servants, and the people of the king's provinces, do know, that whosoever, whether man or woman, shall come unto the king into the inner court, who is not called, there is one law of his to put him to death, except such to whom the king shall hold out the golden sceptre, that he may live: but I have not been called to come in unto the king these thirty days. And they told to Mordecai Esther's w o r d s.   T h e n   M o r d e c a i commanded to answer Esther, Think not with thyself that thou shalt escape in the king's house, more than all the Jews. For if thou altogether holdest thy peace at this time, then shall there enlargement and deliverance arise to the Jews from another place; but thou and thy father's house shall be destroyed: and who knoweth

**whether thou art come to the
kingdom for such a time as
this?"**
- Esther 4:1-16

Mordecai would not back down but turned the
heat further, coming in harder on her. It was
dangerous for Esther to do nothing; she would
not be safe in the palace either by the time she
ended up being the only Jew left. It would only
be a question of time before someone asked
some questions and unsavory answers would
be given. Likely she would have had to die too
since the King had signed the bill to
exterminate them all. We saw this happen with
Daniel in the matter of the lions' den – these
laws were absolute. Also, this king had just
put away his beautiful wife because the
kingdom ethics required him to do so.

Esther declared a three-day fast and sent a
message for Mordecai to call all Jews to join
her. She even promised that her maidens in the
palace would do the same!

Yes, these were the same ladies she was once
feared about facing up to. We can see her
impact growing in the palace having been
there as an emissary of God. She was not only

able to make stately demands of 'her' girls now, but she could impact them to join her in something as deeply personal – not to talk challenging – as a three-day fast for her survival. I guarantee this could not be the first time they would be exposed to her doing things like this. Having been in the palace perhaps a few months or years by now, these ladies would perhaps have been watching their new queen and finding out that she was different. She wasn't the partying type like Vashti; she was quiet, observant, obedient to her husband and elders, caring for that old Jewish man at the gates, tender to her maids, and prayerful too. Likely she had observed a few fasts in that palace too, and by now the idea was no longer alien to them.

Ye are the salt of the earth, folks. You are there to impact and effect positive change on your environment, not to be subdued by it. People around you need to see your light shining and be gravitated toward your Father in heaven because of the person that you are. You have got to understand and embrace this monumental responsibility and then play that role, otherwise you become an unprofitable servant, and unfruitful branch, salt without savor, to be cut down or cast into the street and trodden under the foot of men.

And speaking on fasting... even in the Old Testament it was tantamount to praying seriously, afflicting your body so that you can better hear from God because you want God to miraculously show up in the case at hand. Life demands these actions and we cannot shy away from them, especially when push comes to shove and situations are thrust upon us. Esther prayed seeking heaven's counsel and wisdom. She needed to be reassured of Heaven's backing. After all, "for waging war you need guidance, and for victory many advisers"(Proverbs 24:6).

> *Matthew 7:7-8 further says: "Ask and it will be given to you; seek and you will find: knock and the door will be opened to you. For everyone that asks receives, he who seeks finds: and to him who knocks, the door will be opened."*

This is a kingdom tool, and not one that we should carelessly discard. Any sphere of life you find yourself in, you can and should learn to seek God with all sincerity of purpose, and fasting helps to mortify your flesh and put you in the right mood. For the record, the fasting is not to impress God – it really doesn't do much in that regard; it is to break yourself down to a place where you are more receptive to God.

Are you about moving from that building to another? Getting a better education? Getting married? Trying to save your marriage from a complete break down? You want to stay employed? Do you still blame your dad, mum, or relation for terrible things happening in your life? You might want to rethink all that and ask yourself if you have truly given it all it takes in the place of prayer. Avoid buck passing!

Esther here took a decision to act with faith – an action in the right direction, in spite of the pressure. Understanding that prayer and fasting go together (Judges 20:26-27), she got down to business.

Have you considered the power of prayer? There is no riddle that sincere prayer to God cannot solve, more so with a broken and a contrite heart. The word says, "Call unto me in the day of trouble, and I will show you great

335

and mighty things." I have a feeling it means exactly what it says.

Just get going as you are led
> *"You guide me with your counsel, and afterward you will take me to glory."*
> -   **Psalm 73:24**

Alleluia!
It is pertinent to follow God's leading especially when you have asked for it, otherwise, it is useless if you do not respond to His leading. Esther stood up and walked up to the king at the risk of her very life, trusting that the God she had pleaded with to take charge of the situation will take charge of the situation. Well, if God had not taken control of the situation, she would be dead. Rather she was welcomed.

You and I can likewise take charge of the pressure that comes in life by being quiet and calm, following the Spirit of God and acting by faith.
> *"Now it came to pass on the third day that Esther put on her royal apparel, and stood in the inner court of the king's*

336

house, over against the king's house: and the king sat upon his royal throne in the royal house, over against the gate of the house. And it was so, when the king saw Esther the queen standing in the court, that she obtained favor in his sight: and the king held out to Esther the golden sceptre that was in his hand. So Esther drew near, and touched the top of the sceptre. Then said the king unto her, What wilt thou, queen Esther? and what is thy request? it shall be even given thee to the half of the kingdom. And Esther answered, If it seem good unto the king, let the king and Haman come this day unto the banquet that I have prepared for him. Then the king said, Cause Haman to make haste, that he may do as Esther hath said. So the king and Haman came to the banquet that Esther had prepared. And the king said unto Esther at the banquet of

> *wine, What is thy petition? and it shall be granted thee: and what is thy request? even to the half of the kingdom it shall be performed. Then answered Esther, and said, My petition and my request is; If I have found favor in the sight of the king, and if it please the king to grant my petition, and to perform my request, let the king and Haman come to the banquet that I shall prepare for them, and I will do tomorrow as the king hath said."*
> - *Esther 5:1-7*

Well, even at that the pressure was not over; Esther was not yet home and free but still needed to be wise about how she moved forward. She took her time inviting her husband to dinner, with Haman, twice!

You have got to be as wise as a serpent but harmless as a dove, as the Bible enjoins. Don't just go barging into situations with half-thought out ideas and get yourself injured or killed in the process. Honestly, the battle we face daily is not for us because God fights for us. You can never say where He will draw the line or pull out the joker, so at each point you must put in your utmost. Ours is to be courageous and pray, and then act in faith. Be men of the spirit.

You would not imagine that the king would not be able to sleep, disturbed and searching his heart to see whom he had not recompensed. But the Bible says the "the heart of the king is in God's hands and He turns it withersoever he wishes."

God stirred the king up and things started to change!

Check your heart

> *"On that night could not the king sleep, and he commanded to bring the book of records of the chronicles; and they were read before the king. And it was found written, that Mordecai had told of Bigthana and Teresh, two of the king's chamberlains, the keepers of the door, who sought to lay*

hand on the king Ahasuerus. And the king said, What honor and dignity hath been done to Mordecai for this? Then said the king's servants that ministered unto him, There is nothing done for him.

"And the king said, who is in the court? Now Haman was come into the outward court of the king's house, to speak unto the king to hang Mordecai on the gallows that he had prepared for him. And the king's servants said unto him, Behold, Haman stands in the court. And the king said, Let him come in. So Haman came in. And the king said unto him, what shall be done unto the man whom the king delight to honor? Now Haman thought in his heart, to whom would the king delight to do honor more than to myself? And Haman answered the king, For the man whom the king delight to

honor, Let the royal apparel be brought which the king is accustomed to wear, and the horse that the king rides upon, and the crown royal which is set upon his head: And let this apparel and horse be delivered to the hand of one of the king's most noble princes, that they may array the man withal whom the king delight to honor, and bring him on horseback through the street of the city, and proclaim before him, Thus shall it be done to the man whom the king delight to honor. Then the king said to Haman, Make haste, and take the apparel and the horse, as thou hast said, and do even so to Mordecai the Jew, that sit at the king's gate: let nothing fail of all that thou hast spoken. Then took Haman the apparel and the horse, and arrayed Mordecai, and brought him on horseback through the street of the city, and proclaimed before

him, Thus shall it be done unto
the man whom the king delight
to honor. "
-        ***Esther 6:1-11***

How desperately wicked is the heart of a man! Hamman assuming it had to be him the king wanted to bless, proudly prescribed a recipe for his own shame, a precursor to his doom.
Folks, you need to check your heart too. Don't be so quick to conclude on other men – many of us are just as wicked. Haman was not the first or only person in scripture to prescribe his own doom; even our beloved King David at one time ended up judging himself over the matter of Uriah and Bathsheba. And his ancestor, Judah, ended up impregnating his own daughter-in-law while trying to be crafty. See? Even good men have been caught in bad places before!

You have got to be sober minded if you will ever succeed in walking with God. Do not wish your enemies dead, but pray for them, bless them, and do well to them always. A child of God should never plan evil for people even in those desperate moments – that is the true mark of Godlike character. "Whoso

342

diggeth a pit shall fall into it."When you wish people evil, it tends to come right back at you. This is why you should always allow God to do your battle the way He chooses to handle them, and He will bring forth your righteousness as the light and your judgment as the noonday.

Dr. Patrick Odigie is a man graced with prophetic insights, revelations, and his ministry is marked by signs, wonders, and demonstrations of the Spirit. The Ministry of this Apostolic Prophet, spanning three decades, has taken him to four Continents and he is mandated by God to mobilize the Praying Power of the Church to unleash end-time revival now and Healing of the Nations. Patrick Odigie functions under a powerful anointing of Counsel, revelations, dreams interpretations and encounters in the spirit realm. He is a trained Deliverance minister, substance abuse counselor and a consultant/participant at World Forum of Drug Demand Reduction, Bangkok, Thailand, in December 1994 under the auspices of United Nations Drug Control Program for Non-Governmental Organizations. Brother Odigie is an alumnus of the prestigious Haggai Institute of Advanced Christian Leadership, Maui, Hawaii.

He presently resides in Uniondale New York where Heand his wife, Rev. Mabel Odigie,

Oversees the Prophetic Power house Ministries; and travels extensively throughout the Nation mobilizing churches and Christian fellowship groups to unleash the power of the praying church for end-time healing revival. The three cord focus of his message is Prayer, Sacrifice, and Intimacy with the Holy Spirit as pre-requisites for accessing the power of God for the end-time healing revival. He sees himself as an extreme lover of Jesus, and seeks to promote a spirit of bridal love for the Lord everywhere. Patrick is married to his best friend, Pastor Mabel Odigie, and is blessed with three anointed and prophetic children; Praise, Honor and Favors.

OTHER BOOKS BY
THE AUTHOR

- Foundations for True and Complete Deliverance
- Warriors Guide on Effective Deliverance Ministry
- War is Normal
- Deliverance That Works
- Destiny Under Fire
- The Anointing of The Curse Breaker
- Prophetic Gateways

BIBLIOGRAPHY

1. Jakes, T.D Instincts: The power to unleash your inborn Drive. New York. Faithwords Hachette Book group, 2014

2. Excerpts from Experiencing the Resurrection. Multhomah book. BlackBoy

3. The Telegraph News from Africa. 12th October, 2017.

4. channel.nationalgeographic.com/killing-jesus/articles/how-did-the-apostles-die/

5. MCSPA - BEING HAPPY... (Unknown Author) You may have ...

6. https://www.facebook.com/mcspa/posts/10153625162832490

7. Paul J. Meyer: Unlocking Your Legacy Thomas Nelson Inc, 1982

8. https://www.wikipedia.org/

9. Got Questions
   https://www.gotquestions.org